T0156837

What Now?

A Memoir of Self-Realization

PATTY BIALAK

iUniverse, Inc.
New York   Bloomington

What Now?
A Memoir of Self-Realization

Copyright © 2010 Patty Bialak

iUniverse books may be ordered through booksellers or by contacting:

iUniverse
1663 Liberty Drive
Bloomington, IN 47403
www.iuniverse.com
1-800-Authors (1-800-288-4677)

ISBN: 978-1-4502-6096-1 (pbk)
ISBN: 978-1-4502-6097-8 (cloth)
ISBN: 978-1-4502-6098-5 (ebk)

Library of Congress Control Number: 2010913922

Printed in the United States of America

iUniverse rev. date: 10/12/2010

To my family of friends who never doubted me, who encouraged me at every turn, and who always showered me with love, I remain gratefully in your debt.

I didn't win light in a windfall, nor by deed of a father's will.
I hewed my light from granite, I quarried my heart.

In the mine of my heart a spark hides—not large, but wholly my own. Neither hired, nor borrowed, not stolen—my very own ...

From "I Didn't Win Light in a Windfall" by Chaim Nachman Bialik, CH. N. Bialik Selected Poems (Israel: Dvir Co., Ltd., 1981), 30.

Contents

Preface

Because of the personal and intimate nature of my story, I changed, omitted, and obscured many of the names. In some cases, I did use the actual name, but only when I believed there was no reason not to. Some of the e-mails and letters are paraphrased because they either are a combination of several correspondences or some of the information wasn't relevant to the story. In any case, there is no distinction throughout as to whether the name is real or imaginary or whether the correspondence is complete or edited.

The stories are true. Some of the dialogue is either my best recollection or embellished for creative emphasis.

Introduction

We all have adventure in our hearts, some as a fantasy and some as a motivation to act. For daring folks, my dance through life's travails will make you smile with empathy, and for those of you more likely to listen with rapt attention to your friends' adventures with no desire to imitate, I share my journey in the hope that you will respond with a different sort of empathy. You might recognize that we are all connected and life's challenges feel similar, whether escaping a Tunisian interrogation or dealing with a screaming baby. Disappointment in love is just as difficult to deal with whether you're married to one person for fifty years or date fifty people for one year each. Who's to say whose journey is more difficult?

So, who am I? And why would you be interested in what I have to say? To start with, I'm a member of a generation that changed the world. I am a baby boomer. When our mothers and fathers returned from World War II, they wanted a home and family to wipe out the memories of war. For some, it proved to be the balm they searched for, and for others, nothing would ever fill the hole. At this writing, we are seventy-eight million strong.

I was on the cutting edge of the women's movement and a leader of the sexual revolution. Imagine (or remember) a time when no one knew about STDs, AIDS didn't yet exist, and our only fear was of an unwanted pregnancy. As if by magic, we were given "the Pill." Not only did it prevent pregnancy, but the hormones increased breast size and caused weight gain. I went from a scrawny eighty-five pound, five-foot-three eighteen-year-old to a sensual, sexy, 105-pound woman. We leapt from our parents' era of sexual repression to total freedom with ease and abandon. We were, and still are, a force to be dealt with. Whenever I meet someone my age, I immediately wonder what they were doing in the sixties and seventies. "Drugs, sex, and rock and roll" is not an empty phrase. Anyone who was alive during this era who says they weren't at least aware of these things is either lying or deluded. Rock and roll added fuel to the fire in a psychedelic age, and marijuana was definitely the drug of choice. While our parents used alcohol and prescription drugs to self medicate, many chose a more natural way of softening the relentless images of war, feelings of frustration over all kinds of discrimination, and engaging in recreation without the hangover and unsightly vomiting. Some of us lived through that time of revolutionary change adapting to the new social mores only to regress, as we aged, to become the people we most rebelled against. Many of us never stopped being political activists and continued to work for the downtrodden and unrepresented among us. Regardless of where we each landed, we shared a time that changed who we were and flavored who we were to become.

Boomer women stayed single longer. With more women staying single for indefinite periods of time, it became socially acceptable for a single woman to be sexually active. I know I'm not alone in how I've lived my life. I didn't invent sex, but women of my generation were the first to explore their sexuality without peer judgment.

I tried marriage several times, but the knowledge that I could just as easily make it on my own made choosing other options when the marriages were less than blissful an easy way to go. In my mother's generation, being single was a pox upon her house. In my generation, there is nothing unusual about a person of any age, of any sexual orientation and any appearance, going online to meet people, date, and have intimate relations of any type whenever it feels right. I am a member of the first wave of baby boomers. I represent the group that experienced our entire adult lives going where no one had ever dared to go before. Once the rules of convention had been shed, there was no turning back—at least for me.

Chapter 1
We Are Not All Created Equal

HERE'S MY STORY. My reluctance to tell it is not because it's more horrible than the stories of many other more unfortunate souls but because I fear that I'll be defined by my past instead of who I've become and who I'm yet to be. I've put most of my childhood behind me, but now and then, there are little flashbacks that sneak up and surprise me with the power they still hold over me. I learned years ago how to change my focus, to be positive and to let the past go, but maybe the telling of it is the catharsis that will let me put it away, never to be told again, and finally, to never revisit it.

In the beginning, there was World War II, and as so many couples did in those years, my parents met, quickly fell in love, and married. My mother met a man with whom she had absolutely nothing in common—no intellectual connection, no social connection, nothing but the best sex she had ever hoped for. They married just before he shipped out, and of course, again, right along with many women of marrying age at that time, she was pregnant.

Her next decision would set the course of events for the rest of our lives. How could she know what a price she would pay? And how could any of us, my father, my sister, and I, protect ourselves from what was to come? My mother tried to abort my sister by taking quinine, and for the rest of her life would blame herself for my sister's mental illness, and thus, happiness was not something that was allowed in our home. Guilt was at the root of all decisions, and it permeated our home like the smell of a dead rat buried deep in a wall. It was the common belief at that time that quinine stimulated uterine contractions. Although the truth is that quinine has little, if any, effect on those contractions until regular labor begins, that didn't stop the old wives' tale from persisting. In addition, there is no actual scientific evidence that taking quinine when pregnant can cause mental illness in the fetus. But guilt colored all future deeds.

And we were all destined to do penance. I didn't discover why we lived with so much sadness until years later when my father spilled the beans and casually dropped the bomb. "Your mom never got over the guilt of trying to abort Gail. She took large doses of quinine and soaked in hot baths. I was leaving for overseas, and she was terrified of being left behind with a baby. When Gail developed schizophrenia, your mom was convinced that it was her fault for trying to abort her, and she dedicated her life to making it up to Gail." My father made the disclosure as though it was the most normal, run-of-the-mill explanation of how to bake a cake. Just add one cup quinine and two tablespoons hot water, and season to taste with guilt.

So off to war my father went. He was a man with a tenth-grade education who was briefly trained to be a medic and sent to invade North Africa. Our government doesn't dish out its bad news equally. At the beginning of the war, there was no limit to the time soldiers stayed on the front lines, and my father had the honor of serving there for eighteen months. During this time, he lost all connection to his feelings, his humanity, and all forms of emotion. He didn't become physically abusive; his emotional cruelty was more devastating, though. He simply wasn't there for any of us. He did things that were unbelievably cruel—not because he meant to be mean, but because he had absolutely no empathy. He was unpredictable in his meanness and could go from adoring father to cruel monster on a dime. And he did.

When my father returned from the war remote and emotionally unavailable, my mother decided that a baby would solve their problems, that it would give them something in common, make my father intelligent and articulate, and make him love her in the way she wanted to be loved. She hoped that I would fill a hole in her heart. In the late forties and early fifties, divorce wasn't supposed to be an option. Divorced women were social outcasts, and there were no self-help books available to work out all of the frightening options. So, when my father came back from the war, after a year in a VA hospital for "battle fatigue," they made me. I was their "love child," except I didn't fix a thing.

My sister started acting out at a very young age, and when she hit twelve, her schizophrenia was full blown. I was nine and shared a bed with a sister who hallucinated, raved, saw demons and bugs crawling on the walls, and ran around naked, screaming at her tormentors whenever they appeared. By this time, my parents had separated a few times, and each time my mom would empty out the bank account, throw my father's clothes on the lawn, and create some other drama that would scare the wits out of my sister and me. In spite of Gail's insanity, she was still my big sister, and I adored her. She beat me up, humiliated me in public, and did whatever she could to subjugate me, but still, I loved her. We shared this strange world where adults were unavailable and locked in their own world of fear, shame, anger, and frustration. She found a way to get their attention, albeit negative, which left me totally and completely invisible.

At nine, I had no accountability, no rules, and only vague parental ranting when I did something that some outsiders considered wrong. But as long as I didn't bring anyone from the outside into the game, I could come and go and do as I pleased. About this time, my mom's mother died. I believe that is when everything changed. My mother no longer had any parental pressure to guide her behavior. Her mom had been the center of her world, and now she was cast out to sea without a rudder. This is also when my parents divorced. My mom was working full time, and my sister was hospitalized on the locked ward of the Wayne State Mental Hospital on a regular basis. My mom and I dutifully went to visit each visiting day, and that's where I saw what insanity really is. In the early fifties, shock treatment and very heavy medication were the regimen of the day. My sister's brain was fried and drugged, and the friends she brought home were usually her buddies on short leave from the institution. When I saw the movie *One Flew over the Cuckoo's Nest*, it felt somewhat nostalgic.

By nine, I started waking up in the middle of the night to walk the streets for hours. I had so much on my mind, even then. I worried whether I would become insane like my sister. I wondered what would become of me if my mother just ran away in one of her angry rages. I was such a sweet-looking innocent that most people didn't bother me. The streets were pretty deserted at three or four in the morning, and interactions with strangers were rare. The police would stop me and drive me home, but they never woke up my mom. They just shook their heads in disbelief that I chose to wander the streets of Detroit in the middle of the night. With my angelic charm, they couldn't resist my heartfelt request for privacy, and they would routinely drop me off at the corner of my block so as not to disturb my family. Wandering the streets was a habit that stayed with me.

I was very isolated and had little adult contact, but I did have a best girlfriend, Juanita. And we spent a lot of time together. We made our own world, as young girls do. We discovered boys, told each other our secrets, and giggled all night when we had sleepovers, which, of course, were always at her house. One day I got ready to ride my bike to her house, and my mom asked me where I was going. I told her, and she said, "Oh, they moved away." Many years later, after spending a lifetime trying to figure out what I did to make them "move away" without so much as a, "Fare thee well," it came to me. My mother thought I was a lesbian.

If my memory serves me correctly, at my last sleepover at Juanita's house, she and I were showing each other how we kissed boys. This was not a sexual experience between us. We were showing off. She wasn't sexual about it, and I wasn't sexual about it. It was show and tell. Apparently, her mother or father must have overheard and been shocked and called my mother. My mother's way of dealing with something of that magnitude was to lie. And now there were none. My loneliness was suffocating. I remember, from that day on, there was an orchestrated push to feminize me. I started ballet lessons. I started acting lessons. And she took away my only friend. Am I more feminine today because of it? I doubt that one's sexuality is so easily influenced.

By the time I was about ten or eleven, my hormones were just starting to kick in. I had bizarre dreams of being kidnapped, tied up, raped, and ravaged. It was always guys on motorcycles who were very similar to the guys my sister was hanging out with. Sometimes it was Elvis. What can I say, other than that I was a creature of the times in which I lived? By the time I was twelve or thirteen, when I went for my walks, I got in cars with strange guys. By some miracle, I wasn't murdered. I never had sex. I was a tease. I just wanted to have some human connection. I didn't understand that I was so disconnected from the human race that this was my feeble attempt to be touched and held, and as misguided as it may seem now, cared for. Although I remained a virgin, I became adept at blow jobs, hand jobs, and rubbing against anything to get that wonderful sensation that I'd come to really want. I didn't know that I was having orgasms. I didn't know what I was doing, but I was driven to do it. Sometimes I'd get slapped around when I refused sex and sometimes worse, but I was Clintonesque in my definition of sex, and I stuck to my guns with a fanaticism that could have easily gotten me killed.

By fifteen, we had moved more times than I can count, and I'd gone to more than ten schools. I was working as a car hop for a local Big Boy restaurant and living as an adult in a world that was a total mystery to me. My recurring dream was going to school and forgetting what class I was going to and where it was and of course, the classic dream of noticing I was naked or having all my teeth fall out, or, frequently, of being paralyzed and unable to move, wake up, or save myself. All these I've since learned are classic. But at the time, they were constant and frightening, and I was convinced that they were precursors to my eventual insanity. I would be insane like my sister, and it was just a matter of time. I waited for insanity to come every day of my life until I was thirty-one, when I finally understood that I was okay. If I wasn't insane yet, I probably wasn't going to be. I look back in sorrow at all those years lost to that secret fear. Even to this day, when I find myself overreacting to some slight or feeling angrier than the act against me might deserve, I wonder if it isn't some ingrained genetic reaction. That's not to say that my behavior throughout my adult life hasn't bordered on neurotic on more than one occasion. But then, who among us can say they've never fallen back on what they learned from their parents when there is no other behavior in their emotional repertoire?

My grades in school were exceptional. I'd been an A student all of my life, and books were the wings on which I could, from time to time, fly away. And then, my parents decided to remarry—well, not just remarry, but remarry and move to California where my father was now living. Oh well, what's a little more change? Nobody was interested in what all this was doing to me. As anyone could have predicted, the happy couple lasted one semester. My poor sister was so out of her mind during this time that I've blocked out most of her psychotic episodes. Then, just as abruptly as we came to California, back to Detroit we went. Unfortunately, the semester in the San Fernando Valley near Los Angeles produced all A's without my ever opening a book. I gave absolutely no attention to anything going on in school. When we returned to Detroit, I was behind in my classes, now more than half-crazed with adolescence and hormones, rebelling and acting out, and still, no one noticed.

The day I turned sixteen, I quit high school, and the day I quit high school, my mother made me move out of the house. Although I rarely went home, preferring to spend my time with whichever friends' parents were willing to put me up for months on end, my safety net, flimsy as it was, was now officially gone. What was she thinking? Was this a misguided attempt to get me out of the house and away from the influence of my sister? Or am I giving her more credit than she deserves? I'd like to believe she at least thought she was doing it for my own good. And so, there I was, sixteen years old, living in my imaginary world without a single social skill and without any identifiable view of myself other than that of an invisible person more alone than if I'd been dropped on an island in the middle of an ocean.

Initially, I rented a room in an elderly woman's house and started working full time as a waitress at Big Boy's, but it took only a few weeks for me to go back to school via adult education and complete two years of high school in six weeks. I was motivated after the head cook approached me and invited me to work as one of his "girls." He told me, "A virgin is worth a fortune." My intellect and ability to analyze has been my one saving grace throughout my life. No matter how emotionally lost and beaten down by the world I may have been, my brain never stopped processing and analyzing. I thought, *I can only be a virgin once, and who gets this fortune?* Somehow, I knew it wouldn't be me.

Finally, I turned eighteen, and I was eager to marry. I wanted Ward Cleaver to take care of my every need. For those of you who don't remember who Ward Cleaver was, you may well be much more grounded in realistic romantic expectations than are I and nearly all women of my generation. Ward and June Cleaver were the patriarchs of a sitcom called *Leave It to Beaver*. The parents were squeaky clean and perfect. They were rational in all things and expected their sons, Wally and Theodore, to be clean and well behaved. The younger son, Theodore, or the "Beaver," as he was called, was the mischievous ten-year-old who explored everything, ignored convention, and lived in a way that every ten-year-old dreamed of mimicking. This fifties sitcom set up a generation of young people to imagine that this was real, achievable, and desirable. My entire adult life has been spent fighting this image in creating my own persona. It has not been easy.

Between my mother's constant drama, and my father's emotional absence and abuse, I was never able to identify what it was I really wanted for myself but rather was left to chase a dream of television fantasy that replaced the very real need for parental guidance. I married a short order cook from the restaurant and was very surprised to find that this was not happily ever after. Sex took about two minutes. For reasons that I couldn't fathom, he had male friends spend the night. They slept on the Murphy bed, and I slept across the room on the couch. I was somewhat relieved, though, since he never wanted sex when he had a friend over.

Very soon after we married, I stopped getting out of bed. I stopped cleaning house. I stopped doing much of anything. I hid the dirty laundry in the closet and ignored the dishes in the sink. I stopped going out. I stopped functioning. Today we would recognize these symptoms as depression. The response I got from my husband was a variety of yelled obscenities, or he'd have a "blackout" and attempt to strangle me. I was smart enough to know that this was a bad thing. The first time, I forgave him. The second time, I started considering ways to escape.

At the same time, one of the wives of one of his overnight visitors phoned me and explained what our husbands were doing. Wow, I couldn't believe men did that. I didn't have a clue. But once I knew, I moved out. I was eighteen, divorced, and beyond lost. Time spent in the marriage: three months.

I passed the entrance exam to Wayne State University with no preparation and no problem. I ended up in a commune just off campus in downtown Detroit, and this is where I first encountered marijuana. Thank goodness there were no hard drugs around that early in the "hippie" movement. And thank goodness I had a major phobia of needles when harder drugs did begin to appear on the scene. There was no high on earth that could motivate me to stick a needle in my body. It was 1965. I was a teenager, divorced, sexually baffled, and afraid of everyone and everything. My car insurance was canceled because divorced women at the time were assumed to be loose. The insurance agent said that I was canceled because the insurance company wouldn't be able to control how many drunken men I would allow to drive my car. Insurance companies haven't improved a lot, but at least this kind of profiling has become a thing of the past.

The next seven years were a blur. I explored my sexuality, joined the women's movement, and began to become aware that there was more to life than I was experiencing. Nixon was president, and Watergate was just beginning. I was somewhat active in the peace movement, and I did my share of demonstrating and picketing. At some point, I got deeply in debt and totally disillusioned, and I desperately looked for an escape. I took a guided group tour to Europe (on credit, of course), and came home enthusiastic for the first time about history, culture, and the possibility for adventure someplace other than Detroit. I sold everything I didn't own and left again for Europe, this time on my own without any tour guides.

Mom and Dad's wedding picture, April 20, 1942

Dad holding me, and Gail standing in front of Mom,
at our home on Muirland, Detroit, Michigan

My dad and me when times were good

Patty, the ballerina, posing for the camera

Chapter 2
The L-shaped Room

THE TRAIN PULLED into the deserted station, and I stepped out into the unnaturally bright lights as I paused to glance around and get my bearings. I recognized the word "taxi" on a sign that pointed out into the dark night, and just as I dragged my two over-packed bags to the designated area, a cabbie in a battered vehicle pulled up, leaned over, and yelled something out of the passenger window. What he said was unintelligible, more because I don't speak French than due to any speech defect on his part, but it didn't take a genius to figure out that he wanted to take me to my destination. I looked up at the station clock and saw it was nearly midnight, and the only place I had to go was a pension listed in the travel guide *Europe on $5 a Day*. I had just arrived in Nice, France, circa 1972.

"*Un moment, s'il vous plais*," I glibly responded as I opened my guide book to the chapter titled "Cheap" and pointed to the address listed under the cheapest of the cheap. He smiled knowingly and happily chirped, "*Oui, oui, mademoiselle.*" I jumped in and realized for the first time since I'd arrived that my head was pounding with what promised to be a severe migraine. The taxi ride was endless. If I hadn't been so sick to my stomach and nearly flattened by the pain in my head, I might have taken some interest in the sights, but as it was, I could barely keep from vomiting as we sped through the narrow streets. Eventually, after nearly an hour, we pulled up to a dark, dank building on a dark, dank street, but I could already feel the clean, cool sheets and the soft pillow supporting my miserable head.

To add to my misery, I realized (more honestly, I was completely fixated on this fact during the entire ride) that I hadn't converted any money into francs. I didn't have a clue what the exchange rate was, but I figured everyone took dollars. I no longer cared if I got cheated; I just wanted to get off this endless stretch of road called today and sleep well into that promise of tomorrow. When I waved a ten-dollar bill at the cabbie, he adamantly shook his head and yelled, *"Non! Non!"* and motioned with his hands that he needed more, maybe even much more. I put a twenty-dollar bill next to the ten, and he smiled happily. Grabbing them both, he drove away while I was half in and half out of the vehicle, throwing me and my bags to the curb in front of what I hoped would be my new residence.

With blood dripping down my leg from a badly scraped knee, I rang the bell at the front door and waited and waited. Panic was beginning to take over all of my bodily functions. I couldn't think clearly anymore. The street was deserted and dark. It was now nearly 1:00 a.m. into my hoped-for tomorrow, but my hopes were being dashed moment by moment. Eventually, I tried to open the front door. I'm sure if I'd been rested, I would have done this sooner, but I now had excruciating pain in my leg joining the excruciating pain in my head, so when the door opened easily in my hand, I now also felt humiliation at my own stupidity.

The door opened onto a dark, narrow hallway that led to a dark concierge desk. As I dragged myself and my bags toward the desk, I noticed a body lying on the floor in front of the desk. My heart stopped beating. I stopped breathing. I don't know how long I stood there, but I kept searching my mind for the appropriate response and nothing happened. Finally, I started breathing again, and whether it was foolishness or bravery, I don't know, but I walked up to the body to see if it was dead or alive. The first thing I noticed was that it stank. The smell of some cheap liquor almost knocked me over as I peered over the lifeless body. Then, without warning, the corpse opened its eyes, sat up, and I swear, proceeded back to his desk as though absolutely nothing unusual had transpired.

Registration was nonexistent. He merely grabbed a key, held up three fingers, pointed to the number on the key, and pointed up a dark, steep staircase. So far, my experience of Nice was of darkness. The streets, the hallways, and the mood were all so dark. I took the key, faced the stairs, and started dragging my now impossibly heavy bags to their final destination. Together they weighed about sixty pounds, and given the bleeding knee, pounding head, and full day of international travel behind me, I felt like I was climbing Mount Everest in a blizzard. But climb I did.

At the top of the stairs, I dropped my bags and faced my future. The key fit easily into the lock, and the door swung open to the oddest room I'd seen yet in my limited travels through Europe. It was an "L" with a bare, swinging light bulb over a tiny twin-sized bed shoved up against a bare, paint-chipped wall. The small table next to the bed was the only personal touch in the room. The sink and bidet stood bleakly alone in the near emptiness.

Finally, I allowed myself to feel the emotions that were bursting up and exploding through my already pain-wracked body. I sat on the edge of the bed and cried, softly at first and then bitterly, angrily, and noisily. I didn't care who heard me. I didn't care about much of anything but ending the pain. I was alone in this horrible place, so young, broken-hearted from one too many failed relationships, without much money, and sick. What was the point? I threw open my suitcase and started digging through it, flinging the contents every which way until I found the precious pills. I emptied each container as I took inventory of what I had. It was meager, that's for sure. No one could say this was premeditated. I found four sleeping pills that I had been warned to cut into quarters because of their potency, three pills I couldn't identify, but they looked bigger than even the largest vitamin pill, and twelve aspirin. Without giving it even a moment's thought, I threw them down my throat one by one as I drank water directly out of the sink's spout. Fully dressed, I lay down on the bed, not caring or thinking about the ramifications of what I'd just done. I wanted to be unconscious. Dead would be best. Darkness would do. I needed to be without pain, in any case.

The first thing I heard was birds singing. As much as I didn't want to, I opened my eyes and saw the sun streaming into a room that was, in a word, charming. Nothing hurt as I sat up and assessed my situation. The chipped paint was so much less severe in the sunlight that it was almost unnoticeable, and there were several warm and welcoming items in the room that I hadn't noticed in the harsh electric light when I first arrived. A small table with a pretty lamp and a hand-embroidered doily were placed conveniently next to the bed, and there was a lovely old antique *chiffereau* to house my clothes once I picked them up off the floor. I got up and gingerly stepped over my belongings scattered in every direction, gratefully noticing that my leg wound was not nearly as serious as it seemed the prior evening, and pulled back the beautiful lace curtain. My room looked over a garden with an array of flowers and foliage in every gradation of color.

And off in the distance, unbelievably, I recognized the train station clock. It was at most a block away. My indignation quickly turned to laughter when I thought back to that endless taxi ride. I had to give my cabbie credit for creativity and mentally wished him and his family well.

There was a knock at the door, and before I could answer, the maid entered as she brightly and warmly sang, *"Bon jour mademoiselle, bon jour.* Get up, and eat now," all the while smiling. She didn't even react as she tackled my mess and began neatly sorting and folding my belongings and storing them in the drawers of the *chiffereau*. I was fully dressed from the day before and too embarrassed to stay in her way as she attempted to put some order to my few possessions, so I obediently and sheepishly left her to do what she would do.

The dining area was off to the left as I reached the first floor. The concierge desk was now attended by a smartly dressed gentleman who smiled graciously at me and pointed the way to the breakfast room. As I entered, I was overcome by the commotion of conversation and laughter from the fifteen or so people who had already begun eating, all speaking English, laughing, gesturing, and otherwise enjoying the morning. A table with four guys had an empty chair, and I shyly walked over to join them.

"You must be the American who checked in last night! Don't you just love that old drunk who sleeps on the floor? We all feel safe in our beds knowing he's there, that's for sure!" And then they all doubled over in laughter and started sharing their stories of the first time they came back to the pension late at night after a few drinks themselves to find the now-familiar corpse. I joined in the laughter and shared the story of my taxi ride with my table mates. Eventually, other tables joined in and several people offered to show me the sights and fill me in on where I could get whatever I needed. They were almost fighting over me, and it was wonderful. I forgot all about my miseries and my heartbreaks. I couldn't even remember what had made me entertain, albeit briefly and certainly without much conviction, such a dramatic demise. What a difference a day makes.

My new companions were bicyclists from Canada, hell bent on cycling across North Africa. "You must go to Tunis!" was the unanimous mantra. Marcus, the most attractive of all the young men, was also the one in charge. He spoke primarily in the declarative voice. He turned to me and continued conversationally, "We're riding our bikes there. We've been planning this for months. From our research, it should be exotic and beautiful. There's a boat that goes from Genoa to Tunis once a week. It's Danish, I think. It's cheap, safe, and comfortable, or so we hear from our friends who have already done this. We're on our way to Genoa now."

"Really?" I said. But I thought, *Tunis? Why would I want to go to Tunis? What's wrong with this picture?* What I said was, "Maybe that's what I'll do over the holidays. I have to do something besides sit alone in my room."

Chapter 3
Husband Number Two

AFTER MUCH RESEARCH and planning, I booked my transportation on the DFDS Seaways Danish car ferry, the Dana Corona. I intended to board in Genoa, Italy, on Christmas Eve in order to arrive in Tunis, Tunisia, the day after Christmas, thereby alleviating any need to suffer through a lonely holiday on my own. I'd come a long way since the incident in the L-shaped room, but I didn't want to tempt fate by putting myself into a situation I knew would be depressing. I intended to hook up with my Canadian friends who had given me endless instructions, directions, and dates of when and where we would meet in Tunis. Hopefully, we would all arrive within a week or two of each other.

Travel to Genoa by train was uneventful. A short taxi ride to the ship's departure terminal quickly and easily produced my boarding pass. Although I never would have dreamed up this itinerary on my own, now that I had my ticket in hand, I was impatient with anticipation and wanted to get underway immediately. I absentmindedly leafed through a book, making a pretense at reading, when the ship pulled into port. I was amazed at how large it was. I had envisioned a car ferry to be small in stature, without magnitude. It was as though nightfall had come early when the upper decks blocked out the sun, and the boarding platform was dwarfed by the ship's hull. It had four decks, with the crew's quarters down below and the bridge high above. Almost instantly, the belly of the beast was exposed when the plank dropped down and attached the ship to the dock. The six hundred-passenger capacity appeared to have been reached as swarms of people exited. Then one by one, one hundred cars began snaking their way through the crowded streets of Genoa.

Eventually, the all-clear signal was given, and we were allowed to begin boarding. We wouldn't depart for at least three hours, but I was sure I'd be more comfortable getting situated in my cabin than trying to maneuver anyplace else with my luggage. I was mesmerized with the whole choreography of the dance. Ship to dock, passengers out, cars out, passengers in, cars in, tickets taken and cabins assigned, all done effortlessly. When it was my turn to present my ticket and receive directions to my cabin, I was directed to an elevator that would carry me to my quarters. This ship had a casino, a theater, several gift shops, and a concierge. And after a couple of weeks on my own, I was hungry for conversation and human interaction.

I quickly unpacked and left my cabin to explore my new digs. I wandered aimlessly from deck to deck, and bow to stern, hoping to find a place to sit and people watch. Instead I stumbled upon the casino and the next stage of my life. Sitting with his head bent over a disemboweled slot machine was a stereotypical version of the perfect-looking man. He was blonde with a solid build. His eyes were a blue that only Scandinavians possess. And then he smiled, and there was light. There was none of this in Detroit. I had never seen such a beautiful man. And he was looking back at me with an expression that said my exotically dark eyes and hair were just as intoxicating to him as he was to me.

We both said hi at the same time, and laughing self-consciously, we introduced ourselves. We found that between his horrendous English and an occasional word or two in German or Spanish, we were able to communicate only in the most primitive of ways. So naturally we were in bed almost immediately, and I was totally and completely in love by the time we reached Tunis. My naiveté is what I believe has kept me safe and alive all my life. I can't envision myself coming to harm, and so even in the most frightening of situations, my brain simply computes the discomfort but not the danger. It's as though I'm unable to comprehend an ending in which I'm not ultimately just fine, and the world unfolds exactly as I believe it will. So when Jørn and I left the ship in Tunis, and I gave the directions to my Tunisian hotel to the taxi driver, I had a relaxed feeling of happy anticipation tinged with sadness. I wondered how quickly Jørn would forget me once I was out of his sight. We had promised to write and stay in touch until his ship came back to Tunis in two weeks. But a lot can happen in fourteen days.

When we arrived at the very small pension, I had the wherewithal to ask the driver to wait. From the outside appearance, I had already made the mental decision that this wasn't a good thing. It was a three-room house with what appeared to be two rooms for rent. I was shown to my room, and I laughed out loud. I have never been presented with a situation that was more outlandish either before or since. The bed was rumpled and obviously slept in previously. The odor of urine was everywhere. The floor was wood, with a layer of so much sand and dirt that weeds were growing between the slats. Hanging from the low ceiling was but yet another lone light bulb. I thought to myself that it was a good thing this isn't where I landed from the train station in Nice. I would have hung myself from that sorry little light fixture and ended it all.

I looked at Jørn, and he looked at me, and we made a dash back to the taxi. I'd just have to buy another ticket and take the ship to a friendlier place. We arrived back at customs, and Jørn went up ahead with his seaman's pass, and I waited in line. I filled out all of the necessary forms and answered everything honestly. When the form inquired as to the amount of money I had in my possession, I answered, two thousand dollars. When I handed my paperwork to the customs official, he read it, looked me up and down, and pointed off to the side. Another official came over, took my arm, and led me away. Jørn watched all of this from the other side of the barricade. As they led me away, I looked over my shoulder and saw Jørn running onto the ship.

I was led to a small room, and through sign language, I was instructed to sit. Shortly thereafter, another official began interrogating me in Arabic. I kept repeating that I only spoke English, but this didn't seem to be understood, or if understood, was of no interest. Eventually, I was left alone to ponder what would happen next. Lo and behold, not ten minutes later, the door swung open, and in ran Jørn and the captain of the ship. Jørn took one of my arms, the captain took the other arm, and they literally drug me as fast as they could through the barricade, onto the gangway, and into the ship. Just like that, I was rescued.

In retrospect, the Tunisians must have thought I was a drug dealer to have that much money on my person. Being not just a woman, but a woman alone, made me suspicious even without the cash. This was the seventies, after all, and this was North Africa. Once back on the ship, my Prince Charming spent every free minute with me while we cruised for a week on our way to Malaga, Spain. Jørn and I decided I could go to school there. He had heard there was a school where foreigners could study Spanish. It was Generalissimo Franco's policy at that time to require foreigners to also study Spanish culture, history, and literature in addition to studying the language. Jørn would be back every two weeks, and we could take the ship from Malaga to Tangier and then back to Malaga. And in this way, we could see each other for twenty-four hours twice a month. The rest of the time, I'd be staying in the Costa del Sol, just a short bus ride from the resort and tourist town of Torremolinos, studying Spanish by day, and enjoying the tourist life by night. I'd made friends with the purser and the captain, and most of the Danish crew, and as long as I slept in Jørn's cabin, I wasn't required to buy tickets. I was Jørn's girl. Life fell into a delicious routine. I found a really wonderful pension, Carlos Quintos IV, located conveniently across the street from the school. The campus was part of the University of Granada and offered classes to "*estranjeros*" for an intensive twelve-week course of study that required attendance eight hours a day, six days a week, with no other language being allowed but Spanish.

The class was diverse, with students from China, Russia, Germany, and the United States. We were all on equal footing as the instructor taught us through mime. We all had dictionaries that translated from Spanish to our respective languages, and as long as we paid attention, it really did begin to sink in. The morning vocabulary and grammar lessons were followed by a lecture on current events in Spanish, then a lecture in literature relating to a Spanish book we were assigned to read. Next we moved on to a lecture on Spanish culture and more vocabulary to end the day. Within a month, I began to dream in Spanish. Oddly, I couldn't understand anything that was being said, but my dreams were fluent and relaxed, and the Spanish just flowed from mental image to mental image.

We were immediately forced to speak. It was painful to say the least, except that we were all equally bad. The instructor encouraged us to go to the local Tapas bars and drink cheap wine and talk to each other. The wine did the trick. We would all go to the local pub after class every day, and since Spanish was all that we had in common, we'd communicate as best we could, and pretty soon speaking was neither forced nor difficult. As I finished my semester, I had to face the fact that my two thousand dollars had dwindled away. All that I had left was my return ticket home and one thousand dollars. I was going to have to give serious consideration to going home. I wasn't ready. I was in love. And just when I thought all was lost, Clive, one of the other students, asked me if I was interested in working for food and shelter up on top of the hill in Malaga. All I had to do was help him and a friend move wheelbarrows of dirt from one place to another so that he could build a retaining wall. He was remodeling a house for a friend who was away traveling in Europe.

Wow. Would I? You bet I would. My mind was doing the math, and this meant that I could stay much longer. When the taxi dropped me off at the house at the top of the hill, I was speechless. It was a mansion to be sure but in desperate need of repair. Once I was inside, I realized that it was even worse than the outside forewarned. There was no electricity, no heat, of course no air-conditioning, and no running water. We had plenty of candles and blankets and a fresh-water well outside. The bathroom was an outhouse in back. Although the house was under construction and would one day be marvelous, that wouldn't happen for some time.

Still, it was a place to live and work between trips to Tangier and back with Jørn every two weeks. I wouldn't have to use any of my money, since Clive promised to buy the groceries. And I was willing to do almost anything as long as I could remain in Malaga and see Jørn on a regular basis. We coexisted in this rugged environment for a few months. Jørn and I were madly in love and lived in the moment. We both knew this story had a beginning and an ending. We were just trying to prolong it as much as we could. Jørn told me of his plans to go back to Denmark for a few weeks when the ship went to dry dock for annual repairs in Marseilles. When the day arrived, our good-byes were filled with angst and tears as we gave each other our pledge of fidelity. After leaving the ship, I returned to the house on the hill. Clive came home shortly after me and announced to both Clarence and myself, "My lover is coming home next week, and you both have to be gone. He doesn't know about Clarence." And I thought, *Neither did I.* I really did think they were just friends. Do you see the naiveté that just never seems to go away?

I decided I'd go to Madrid by train, stay in a cheap hostel, and take some classes at the University of Madrid until Jørn returned from Denmark. I don't know what I'd hoped would happen, but if I left Spain without talking to Jørn, I might regret it for the rest of my life. I mailed him a postcard for delivery in Genoa and explained that I had to leave the house in Malaga and would be studying in Madrid for awhile. I gave him the address of the hostel I would be staying at from my trusty *Europe on $5 a Day* guide. I warned him that I was running out of money and the future for us looked bleak.

I took the train to Madrid, and when I arrived, the armed Guardia Civil were everywhere around the campus. There had been a student uprising against Franco, and they were shooting students in the street. The hostel turned out to be a private home with six other students. We ate communally, and both room and board really were just about five dollars a day. Registration was surprisingly uneventfully at the university, and I soon began another semester of study. Every day waiting for a reply from Jørn was torture. *Was it just a shipboard fling?* He must meet hundreds of women. *Was it sincere, but unrealistic in the harsh light of day to think it's going to continue?* I was plagued all day every day with thoughts of Jørn and our star-crossed path. Finally, weeks later, I received a postcard.

> Dear Patty,
>
> I love you. Come back to Malaga and get a job on the ship. I'll help you.
>
> Love,
>
> Jørn

I left Madrid the next morning. The outcome was unimportant. Jørn said "Come back." Jørn said, "I love you." I left my classes incomplete and arrived back at the Carlos Quintos IV Pension. I was given a warm homecoming, and it was good to get back to the comfortable, well-run little refuge. I met Jørn at the dock as usual. He came running down the gangplank, took me in his arms, and smothered me in kisses. The nearby Guardia Civil hissed their usual, "*Es prohibito!*" at any public display of affection, and we dutifully withdrew and skipped into the ship and back to his cabin.

The entire twenty-four hours on board were bittersweet. We knew it could be our last. We begged the purser to find some work for me so that I could stay on the ship, and he promised to give it his best. When it was time to leave, Jørn and I waited until they made the final announcement that warned all visitors to go ashore. As he kissed me for the last time, we promised that we'd find a way to get back together. But we both knew it wasn't going to happen. Then, the purser came running up to us, lifted me up, and carried me back into the belly of the ship, where the cars had just filled the void for the next leg of the journey. "You've got a job, Patty! And, you've got a private cabin! Welcome aboard."

Chapter 4
I'm a Seaman

"VENGA! TRAIGALOS LA *ropa de cama y un pozal y una escoba ahora mismo! Venga! Venga! Andeles!" Welcome to Mars*, I thought. I had no idea what was being asked of me, or of the assembled cleaning crew of which I was now a member. I had hurriedly filled out the appropriate paperwork the preceding evening, had received my seaman's identification card, was assigned a cabin coincidentally next door to Jørn's, and now, just twelve hours later, here I was reporting for work. It was very clear, even with the language barrier, that I wasn't welcome. I was an outsider. I was a foreigner. This ship flew a Danish flag, was run by Danish officers, and was managed by Danish employees, with a Spanish cleaning crew. I was neither Danish nor Spanish.

My intensive study of the Spanish language, history, culture, and politics both in Malaga and Madrid did not prepare me for the orders that were now being barked at me. I could order in a restaurant, I could ask for directions, and I could shop with relative ease, but I wasn't prepared for Miguel, who spoke at machine-gun rat-a-tat speed without breath or punctuation. I just stood there silently waiting to be escorted off the ship for misrepresenting that I did indeed speak Spanish. Instead, Miguel, my new boss, pointed to Angel, apparently my new partner, to take me and show me what to do. At least that's what I assumed he said, since Angel then grunted at me, got behind me, and pushed me in the direction of the passenger cabins.

The previous evening had been a whirlwind of paperwork, unpacking, celebrating with the Danish crew, and letter writing to let my mom know where I was and what I was doing.

Dear Mom,

You won't believe how much everything has changed since I last wrote to you. I know I was thinking about coming home because I was running out of money. Well, I have a job. I know! It's amazing. I met the man I'm going to marry. He doesn't know it yet, but he does love me and I love him. I'm working on a ship in the Mediterranean with 102 crewmembers, of which only ten are women. We carry six hundred passengers and a hundred cars and cruise all over the Mediterranean Ocean. We go from Genoa, Italy, to Tunis, Tunisia, to Patras, Greece, to Palma de Mallorca, Spain, to Malaga, Spain, to Tangier, Morocco, then back to Malaga, finally returning to Genoa to complete the route. It takes two weeks to make the trip, and we're followed by a sister ship one week behind us so that each port is serviced once a week.

Believe it or not I'm making enough money to support myself and save some for when the job is over. They pay for all food and board, an extra bonus for weekends, and a salary of four hundred dollars a month. All in all, they will be putting about six hundred dollars a month into a bank account for me, which I can draw down whenever I need it. I plan on leaving the money there and will live on what's left of my money. I don't have many needs, and Jørn pays for everything when we go on leave or when we dock at a port.

My private cabin is small, just a bunk, a chair, a table, and a porthole. But don't underestimate the importance of having a cabin with a porthole. All of the Spanish crew live on the deck below, and they're really in the bowels of the ship. There are no windows, no natural light, just pitch black. I got this cabin because the person who vacated it was airlifted to Denmark near death from alcohol poisoning. He was a Danish engineer, and so his cabin was private, above the water line, and in the area of all the other Danish managers and officers. I even get to eat in the Danish cafeteria because everyone knows that I'm with Jørn, and that we take our meals together. They seem awfully accommodating, so I'm looking forward to having fun in my off hours.

I'm part of the cleaning crew, which I think even I can do, and how much Spanish do I need to clean up after people? I've got a dictionary. I think I'll be fine. So, don't worry about me. I don't know how often letters get sent from the ship, and I don't know when I'll be home. It may be a year, or it may be two years. And maybe, if there are miracles, I won't leave Europe at all. Just know that I'm happy.

Love,

Patty

I may have spoken a little prematurely. I soon learned that the rules for the Spanish crew and the Danish crew were diametrically opposed, and I was officially part of the Spanish crew. We worked a split shift seven days a week. We started at 6:00 a.m. cleaning the public restrooms and lobby areas, and then the passenger cabins had to be cleaned before we could break for lunch. We came back to work after the traditional siesta at 4:00 p.m. When we were at sea, in the afternoon, we just made the beds, cleaned the sink and toilet, emptied the trash, and changed the towels. In port, we changed all of the linen in addition to the other cleaning chores. Angel and I were assigned thirty cabins, and we were able to dash through them with little or no problem. And then after a few days, Angel explained the facts of life to me.

"Patricia, si no me encuentras, diga nada!" And with that, he turned and walked away. Hmmm, he had just instructed me to say nothing if I was unable to find him. So it appeared that I would do everything, and he would do nothing, and I would stay quiet. Later I discovered that he was quite the drunk and spent his days onboard in a haze of alcohol, and quite possibly was on his way to the same demise as my previous cabin occupant. The good news was that he was always present for the changing of the linens. It would be physically impossible for me to change all of the beds on my own. And in this chore, Angel never let me down. I will always remember him kindly for that.

Eventually I got into the rhythm of my job and what was expected of me. I fell into an easy hybrid Spanish that included the verb infinitive if I couldn't remember how to conjugate it. I used whatever tense I could remember and relied on the listener to supply the correct time frame. And most importantly, since Jørn was a member of Danish management, I enjoyed all of his privileges. He only worked while we were actually at sea, since gambling was regulated by international law and forbidden within three miles of port. Each evening at sea, he worked in the casino until 11:00 p.m. and then came back to the cabin. Since the cleaning crew got a wakeup call, or more specifically a cabin door pounding, at 5:00 a.m. with an accompanying, *"Arriba! Arriba! Ahora mismo! Arriba!"*, it was virtually impossible to oversleep. The reason for this forceful morning reveille was because our contracts included a clause that nonappearance at morning roll call resulted in immediate dismissal. I assure you even Angel never missed a roll call.

Since our bunks were so small, Jørn and I would sleep in our own beds in our own cabins at night. I would sit in the casino after work and talk to him while he attended the passengers, selling tokens and periodically fixing broken machines. But mostly we spent those evenings at sea talking. This would be a good time to elaborate on the meaning of the word "talk" as it pertained to Jørn and me. We communicated in a series of disjointed words from various languages, elaborate gestures, and facial expression. As we laboriously made ourselves understood, we discovered that in the simplest of terms, we were both lost and were glad to be found. It was really that simple. And if we never left this place and this time, our love would have been perfect and unending.

The ship went into dry dock every year in Marseilles. The crew had two months off, and for Jørn, that meant going back home to Ahrüs, Denmark. Ahrüs is a small provincial city on the main Island of Jutland. For weeks before the date of our departure for Marseilles, I waited for Jørn to invite me to go to Denmark with him. Where else was I supposed to go for two months? Granted, I now had enough money to pay my way, but so what? Should I go back to Carlos Quintos IV in Malaga and just hang out? There were certainly worse situations to be in, but there was a little bit more to my dilemma than the obvious romantic drama. When we reported for duty after the ship's dry dock maintenance, I would be reassigned to an "appropriate" cabin with the Spanish crew. This meant that I would share a cabin with a crew member in the bowels of the ship and be restricted to the Spanish cafeteria (and after a couple of visits there over the last year, I assure you this was not an option unless carbohydrates, grease, and fat are your foods of choice), and I would be forbidden to go to the deck with the managers and the officers.

After a year on board with the privacy of my own cabin, free access to any crew cafeteria that struck my fancy, and sharing all of my free time visiting with Jørn in the various cabins of the managers and officers with whom we socialized as a couple, to be so extremely restricted on my return made it all really unattractive to me. How in the world was I going to get Jørn to invite me to Denmark and then quit his job on the ship for me? We'd been together now for about a year, and we regularly and frequently announced our love for each other. We were rarely out of each other's sight except when I was working. But still, it would be a huge step, and I couldn't imagine that he was going to just jump onboard, so to speak, and take a job on land and give up the whole seaman gig just for me. I couldn't have been more wrong. All Jørn had to hear was the part about me not being able to come to his cabin, and that I would be sharing a cabin. In his usual direct manner, he simply said, "No."

We went to Denmark together while the ship was in dry dock and spent a couple of months with his family, which consisted of a little brother and sister who found me to be an odd specimen, his parents, and his older sister and brother-in-law. In Denmark, people live at home until they're ninety, or so it appeared to me. Jørn's family was unhappy with his choice of a mate, and they treated me with disdain and distaste; and when Jørn announced that he was going to California with me instead of returning to his job with DFDS Seaways, his parents were silent. Whatever paperwork was required, I've long since forgotten, but somehow there we were. We ended up married by a justice of the peace in Las Vegas, living in a cute one-bedroom apartment in Venice, California, and living together in perfection. Our lives were every bit as perfect as Ward and June Cleaver. Every dream I'd ever dreamed was now true. I had it all, and that included: all the cooking, all the cleaning, all the shopping, sex on demand (but now with no foreplay or concern as to my satisfaction), and a full-time job while Jørn simply went to school. To his credit, after a year, he graduated from a technical school, which, by the way, was taught in English, and had to be quite a challenge for him, and immediately found a job in a business machine repair shop when he graduated.

But again, for different reasons than my first marriage, marital sex was awful. No orgasms. He'd get on, and he'd get off. On the ship, I was often too tired to think about sex, and when we did do it, we were usually in a hurry to get somewhere or meet someone or party with someone, and I was just so happy to be loved that I made excuses and hoped with time it would get better. I somehow came to believe that good sex and a happy marriage were mutually exclusive and that I would have to give up sexual satisfaction to be with someone who fit my mental picture of what a perfect husband should be. Jørn was drop dead cute and sweet to me, and he was totally committed to acting out the "happily ever after" script. I was a "Stepford Wife," and for five years, I baked, cooked, learned Danish recipes, worked, put Jørn through school, and completely left the proverbial building. I had no opinion that didn't come from Jørn's mouth. I had no preference for anything that he didn't prefer. We were joined at the hip. We never fought. We never disagreed. We were perfect. We were perfectly false. We worked at minimum-wage jobs six months a year and traveled six months a year. Life was good. Luckily, there was a shortage of business machine repair people and statistical typists. We were minimally employed at all times we chose to work.

In 1977, I got a phone call from my mom, who announced that she was again leaving my father. She was now in her third marriage to him (or was it her fourth?), and I just couldn't help laughing at her. We got into a fight, and I hung up on her. Hours later, the phone rang and a woman whose voice I didn't recognize asked me if I was Patty. I was surprised because at that time I went by Pat, ignoring my given name, Patty, as childish. "Yes, who's this?" I had already forgotten about the spat with my mom and was preoccupied with other thoughts. "I'm sorry to tell you that your mother has been in an accident, and she's in critical condition. Can you get here right away?"

When I arrived at the hospital, I was immediately directed to where my mother lay. Her eyes were closed and she had tubes in every orifice and a sheet draped over her nearly nonexistent body. I walked over to her bed. No one had prepared me for this, no one was nearby when I approached the bed, and no one could help me when what I saw sunk in. She had been literally driven over by two cars. A very young woman who passed out from drugs at the wheel crossed over the center line and struck my mother's car head on while my mother stood behind it loading the trunk with her belongings to once again leave my father. Two cars had driven over her body, and there didn't appear to be an inch of her that wasn't swollen grotesquely or covered with bandages. My first reaction was to scream, and I did, loudly. And then I whispered, "Ma, can you hear me?" She hated to be called Ma. To her it was what she called her mother, and that meant it was old-fashioned. And my mother was modern. She had thrown off the yoke of Orthodox Judaism and embraced the new and modern Reform Movement of modern American Jews. She was modern beyond the times. She dreamed of a better life for me and encouraged me to push the envelope and follow my dreams. I wasn't able to stop and edit my language. I continued, "Ma, blink if you hear me." Tentatively and slowly, her eyes blinked.

"Ma, I'm sorry. I didn't mean to yell at you. I love you." My mom blinked several times before the nurse arrived to drag me out of there. "Didn't anyone talk to you before you came back here?" She was incredulous that I was allowed to just walk into the intensive care unit without so much as a "howdy do." It took my mom seventy-two hours to die. She never regained consciousness after my short visit with her, and I never went back into her room. I was traumatized. I was guilt ridden. I was stunned. I was twenty-seven. We had had so little time together, and so much of it was angry. I'll always be grateful that I had those sixty seconds to tell her I was sorry and that I loved her. Violence is so random. It's not something that can be planned for.

My father and I made the funeral arrangements, although I was observing everything from someplace outside my body. He behaved as though their marriage was perfect and she was just on her way to the store when she was killed. There was never any mention that she was loading up the car to leave him, and maybe all these years later, I'm willing to give him the benefit of the doubt. But it was eerie to sit and watch him go on and on about his "honey" and how he couldn't live without her, when the result would have been the same whether she had lived or died. I never said anything. Live and let live is my motto.

At the funeral, people began arriving, and all the surviving aunts and uncles were in attendance. My aunt Esther, my mom's sister, had already passed away, as had her youngest brother, Ben. My aunt Ethel had been injured in the same accident as my mom. She was standing off to the side of the car while my mom loaded the trunk. The impact threw her to the curb, while my mom was run over by both her car and the oncoming out of control car. Aunt Ethel was still recovering at home, but my mom's favorite brother, Morris, was there. I never did have any particular bone to pick with him. I didn't see him often, and when I did, he was just part of the family's background noise. I had no idea the venom he harbored toward me.

My sister Gail arrived with her current husband/partner/companion (I don't remember their formal status) who was a famous basketball player fallen from grace by too many drugs and a mean streak that explained my sister's missing front teeth. They had met at a halfway house where my sister was to transition from her most recent incarceration in a mental institution and he from his drug addiction. It was a match made in heaven. It had been many years since I'd seen her, and it was hard to process the changes she had undergone. She had corn-rowed hair in keeping with her current identification with the African American world in which she and her black husband now lived. Her four-foot-ten, eighty-pound frame carried her off-kilter cadence across the mortuary chapel over to me as we shyly embraced. She walked with her head slightly ahead of her torso, as though she was falling forward and moving her feet was an afterthought. It was a typical schizophrenic shuffle, and I had been accustomed to it, but now after such a long absence, it broke my heart. When she smiled, she seemed unaware of how disconcerting her missing front teeth were, and it was with great difficulty that I kept my eyes focused on hers. As the funeral ended and family and friends began leaving the graveside to reassemble at one of the relatives' homes, people came up to me to make small gestures of consolation.

"She's finally happy. Her life was so hard." "I'm so sorry for your loss; I know your mom loved you very much." And the best of all was from my dear uncle Morris, "I hope you're happy now! You killed her! You just abandoned her and went off to God knows where. Well, like I said, I hope you're happy." I stood there silently trying to translate the words my ears heard and find the meaning that they conveyed, but my brain would not or could not process this input. I couldn't envision from where all that hatred had come. What had my mother told him? Didn't he realize that she had thrown me out? I left the cemetery and did not attend any of the family functions. I walked away and never turned back. I never visited my mom's grave and never saw any of the family again until many years later when my sister was murdered.

In the meantime, Jørn was undergoing some radical changes. He had begun to make friends and create his own American persona, and it was offensive. He started hanging out with a bunch of dirt bikers, and he began peppering his speech with sexist, redneck, bigoted comments. As his English improved, I found that we had absolutely nothing in common. While we had struggled for years with broken English and superficial observations, the discovery of a less superficial but completely unacceptable mindset began to present itself. When I would attempt to share my own feelings and observations, I would get an absentminded, *"Ja, ja,"* and that was about as far as I ever got. Shortly after my mother's death and soon after I had returned to college to finish my degree, I had an epiphany. All of a sudden, I understood I wasn't alive. The independent, adventurous, free spirit had died somewhere along the line, and if I ever wanted to feel anything again, I had better run, not walk, to the nearest exit. I understood the marriage was an emotional sham.

I was now back in school and in the process of earning my business degree. I slowly began to learn, to grow, and to get exposure to philosophy, psychology, and sociology. I began getting up at 5:30 a.m. to listen to a public radio program that broadcast lectures by Alan Watts, who spoke about Zen in the sixties and seventies. One particular morning, he was talking about how we're all from the same molecules in this universe, the butterfly, the tree, me, and all humanity. We're all the same. We're all equal. We're all made by God, and we all possess divinity. We are one. I am a tree. I am a butterfly. I am perfect exactly as I am, even with my imperfections.

It was the first time in my life that I understood my own value and worth. It was as with all epiphanies, totally clear and totally mine. I am a butterfly. I am perfect. I am divine, as we all are. Unfortunately, I tried to share this insight at work that day and was fired before the day was over. This was the only time in my life I've ever been fired, but there is truth to the adage that when one door closes, another door opens. I started my own bookkeeping business and made more money and more connections than I ever would have had I remained in that job.

Chapter 5
Just Call Me Eliza (Doolittle, That Is)

EVENTUALLY, I GRADUATED from college and got my first job as a CPA. This is when I met Greg. I was about thirty-three, emotionally about nine, and Greg saw something in me that he valued, admired, and came to love. I saw him as my brother, my mentor, my mother, my father, my friend, my soul mate, and every other human role model. He showed me that one person's love can change everything. His love changed me from the inside out. I was finally redeemed.

When I met Greg, I was lost. To say I was frightened would be like saying World War II was a misunderstanding. I lived in terror—terror that I wasn't smart enough and terror that I would never find someone to love me in such a way that I could love him back. Oh, I'd been loved many times. I'd been loved by strange and distant men who saw in me a product of their imagination. No one saw me. No one loved me. They loved the woman they were hell bent on molding me into. When the pliability of my soul didn't fit the mold of their dreams, disappointment brewed. By the time I met Greg, I was the perfect victim. Paralyzed by fear, I was manipulated and controlled by it. When I met Greg, I was at the end of my rope. Despair would have been a step up.

Freshly graduated from California State University at Northridge January 1, 1980, with a bachelor's degree in business with a major in accounting, I was on my way to a lucrative career as a CPA. My first assignment as a rookie at my first job in a national CPA firm found me at the offices of David B. Goodstein, the philanthropic publisher of the *Advocate Magazine*, the last word in all things gay.

I had been sent out to handle the accounting, all of it, including oil and gas leases, fine art collections, horses, home construction, manufacturing of sexual lubricants, sexual research, and more gay men than I'd ever seen in my life. None of the male accountants at my Century City office were willing to work there, as the culture of Fox & Company, CPAs (since defunct), was white, straight, male, Midwestern, and intolerant of any alternative lifestyles unless it involved wife swapping or sleeping with the secretaries. This was an opportunity that the following twenty-plus years of my career would hinge on. This chance would prove to be the basis of a successful accounting practice, the source of friendship, inspiration, insight, and a sense of family and security that would be there for me for the rest of my life. And somehow, I sensed all that as I walked into that office for the first time. I understood that this was big and I had to pull it off. Greg had just been hired as the bookkeeper, and between the two of us, we barely were able to figure out what it was we were supposed to be doing. The offices had just moved to Los Angeles from San Francisco, and the accountant from the San Francisco branch of my firm had flown down to train Greg and I, and we had one day to understand the workings of a complicated jumble of intertwining entities.

I arrived to the meeting suffering from advanced fibroid tumors in my uterus, which caused the formation of huge blood clots when I had my period. These clots were the size of an embryo and were so numerous that I had to pass one nearly every twenty minutes. The pain was somewhere between excruciating and childbirth. Every twenty minutes, I had to excuse myself, lay down on the bathroom floor, writhing in pain as the clot passed onto paper towels, and then quickly dispose of in the nearby toilet. I was overdosed on pain pills, and at best, the day would be remembered only to the degree I could document the information in my notes. This was going to be a long fucking day.

I had to trust my instincts, and I told both Greg and the CPA training us the truth. I told them that I wanted this assignment more than anything and if they would just teach me in twenty-minute intervals and not tell anyone what was going on, I'd be grateful. Everyone agreed, and that's when Greg and I connected in a way that would change my life forever. Somehow, we all got through that day, and Greg saw something in me that was irresistible to him. Maybe it was his need to control and my need to be controlled. We were a perfect match. He took over my life and began the education of Pat. He was my Pygmalion, I, his Eliza, his clay. But rather than create me in his image, he helped me to create myself into the person I'd always dreamed I could become. He believed in me and was always by my side.

Greg understood that I needed to learn every single human social skill. He patiently taught me how to be a friend. He taught me how to be generous instead of always living in survival mode. He taught me the value of the truth. He really gave me the opportunity to live a life of some value. He taught me ethics, honor, and responsibility. But more than anything, he taught me what it meant to really, unconditionally love someone. And everything he taught me, he taught me by example. He never told me to do anything. He showed me. I'll never know how he understood my need for such gentle treatment. But the combination of his love, the fact that he was gay and had no sexual interest in me at all, and his uncanny understanding that I needed a soft place to land captured my heart and soul, and we became soul mates for fourteen years until his death.

When I became a partner of a West Los Angeles CPA firm, I brought all my questions of ethics home to Greg, and he'd tease me into doing the right thing. My staff had no idea that the reason they were well paid was because Greg wouldn't give me his smile until I answered tough questions about what was really right. I can't deny that Greg was dominating. He was definitely a powerful person. He was the center of our entire family of friends, not just to me, but he used his power for good and not evil. He simply had the capacity to love lots of people and make each one feel like they were very special. Over time, we fell into a comfortable pattern. Initially, Greg would phone me three times a week and most weekends.

"Where are you?" he always asked.

"I'm home, you're calling me," I always said.

"Why aren't you here?" he always responded.

"I'll be there in twenty minutes." And I'd hang up and drive over to his place in Hollywood where he and his partner, Dan, lived.

Eventually, I'd call Greg from work three times a week around 6:00 p.m. "Are you home?" I'd ask.

"Uh, yeah," he'd respond.

"Hanging out tonight?" We both always had an equal option to opt out.

"Yes, come over," he'd almost always respond.

This pattern in various forms continued until he was too sick to call. Dan, his partner, usually went to the gym after work, and Greg and I would sit around listening to music, reading the paper, and talking, or I should say Greg listened. It seemed I could never tell him enough about who I was and what I was doing. If Greg was feigning interest, he deserved an Oscar. We had two hours three or four times a week for fourteen years. When Dan came home, we'd all go out to dinner and then come home and watch our favorite television shows, and then I'd go home. On weekends we'd go to parties, travel or go to the movies, the theater, an opera, or a symphony or just hang out. We were a family of three. Greg and I had a connection that everyone saw, accepted, and understood. It was a love that required no explaining. I would come, over time, to explain it this way. It didn't matter what we did, what we said, or who else was there. As long as we were in the same room, life was as it should be. That's not to diminish in any way the love I felt for his partner, Dan, or obviously, the love Dan and Greg shared. It's just that the initial relationship began with Greg taking me under his wing. Dan and I developed our own deep and enduring relationship, too. But Dan didn't need to show me how to live. We bonded as equals and best friends. Greg would always be my mentor.

When Greg told me he had AIDS, I stopped dating, and if it's possible to imagine, I spent even more time with both Greg and Dan. I came over almost every night after work and most weekends. I wanted to know in my heart that when Greg died, I would have no regrets. It appeared certain that he would die, as medical progress was slow, and once HIV morphed into AIDS, it truly was a death sentence, unlike today with medication available to manage the disease.

It was important to me that there would be no unspoken feelings and no unresolved issues. After experiencing my mother's sudden death, I was sensitive to letting anyone walk away from me in anger. I never wanted to end up in a hospital room with someone I loved and have to remember our last words were limited to blinking. In Greg's case, since we never fought, I wanted to be sure he always knew that my love was unconditional and unending and that I'd be there right up to the end no matter what that end was. We both wanted to be sure there would be complete peace and closure. Many years after Greg's death, I asked Dan if he had ever been sick of me hanging around all the time. He smiled, and said, "Sometimes." And we both smiled lovingly, as I nodded in understanding.

My graduation picture January 1, 1980 from
California State University, Northridge

Me and my dad at our reunion after a long
estrangement, celebrating my becoming a CPA

Greg, Collin, Jim, Dan, and me just hanging out

Greg, Collin, and me on our way to Catalina, with Dan taking the Picture

Greg, Collin, and Dan, Catalina Island

Chapter 6
The Story of Husband Number Three

WHILE GREG WAS deteriorating with debilitating disease after debilitating disease, Dan and I did the best we could to do what had to be done in our day-to-day lives. Greg had been wise enough to have great insurance, and when the time came, he had insurance-paid, around-the-clock home health care. But the stress of watching and waiting for someone you care about to die is excruciating. In the end, my feelings were deeper than just losing a friend. I was losing my brother, my best friend, my mentor, and my spiritual advisor. I had nightmares of disintegrating into thin air. I could feel myself slipping into a very dark depression.

The Internet was just in its infancy. There were dating sites called bulletin boards, and they were very sexual. A friend showed me a site, and I went online and started to chat with men. The board functioned as a predatory place for men. As soon as a woman signed onto the site, someone would send a message and ask if you would talk to them in a "private room." If you said yes, you would click some keys and end up typing back and forth privately in real time via the bulletin board site, very much like today's instant messaging.

Conversations didn't start out with a sexual nuance. That developed slowly over the course of the session. Some people got into computer sex; some people just chatted for a while and then met. It was very much like today's online dating sites, but without the pictures, the detailed profiles, or really the sharing of any personal information at all other than a blind two-way conversation. And that's how I met him. I would go online after visiting Greg in the hospital. I would be so wired that the thought of going to bed and sleeping was out of the question. I could sit at the computer far into the night and distract my mind from trying to formulate what I would do with my life without having Greg there to share it with. He showed up as my knight in shining armor. After I told him what I was going through, he was quick to explain:

> My sister died almost a year ago, and I took care of her at the end. We hadn't even been close. But those last six months meant more to me than anything before or since.

I read his words on the computer screen, and he had me. He was someone who could imagine what I was going through. All thoughts of danger or concern that I didn't know anything at all about this man disappeared. He was my angel. He understood.

We made arrangements to meet in person. When you really think about how random this coupling was, you'll realize that it was all about who was online at the moment I signed in and who was fast enough to invite me into a private chat to get me out of the main chat room chatter. When you compare that to what we do on singles sites online now, refining our searches to include everything from height to weight to hair color to religion to location and on and on, it's amazing. In the old days, almost anyone could meet almost anyone. That explains a lot about how he and I got together. It was simply a random coupling in the universe. It was a cosmic joke.

We agreed to meet in a local deli, and he described himself as good looking with a few extra pounds. We all know what that can mean. It could be anything from literally a couple of extra pounds to obesity. I arrived early so that I could watch the door. I was fully committed to just walking out if I had the feeling this guy was in any way weird. I watched as this somewhat short, chubby guy walked in the door wearing what appeared to be an outdated Nehru jacket with ill-fitting pants, indicating that he had recently gained weight and hadn't yet dealt with the reality. He stood at the entrance scanning the tables, looking for what he hoped would be a hot woman, and as I felt his eyes assess me, I wondered if he was hoping I was her. I decided that he wasn't all that good looking, but nonetheless harmless enough for a cup of coffee. Ladies, you should never rely on appearances. Some disturbed people look like everyone else. He looked okay. He spoke normally. He was not normal. Finally, I looked up and caught his eye. I smiled and indicated that I too was looking for him. He walked over and introduced himself, and the saddest, most hopeless episode of my life began.

Clearly, I'm responsible for any abuse in my life. As hard as I'd worked in developing and nurturing my own self-esteem, there was always someone lurking in the wings to lure me into a needy, emotionally unstable relationship. I'm fodder for the grist. My need for approval and affection and acknowledgment far surpasses all of my intelligent observations and epiphanies. All a man had to say was, "I know what you need. I know better than you. Follow me …" and I was off to the races. Abusive men could smell my need, and they were drawn like a flesh-eating virus to new meat. Once infected, my will was incinerated under the fire of desire and insecurity. He was a master. I had no idea that he had spent years as a counselor with the now-defunct Synanon. He had spent those years training in the fine art of psychological manipulation. Although the concept of Synanon was good on the surface, as he disclosed more and more of the behind the scenes manipulations, it became clear that Synanon was a cult. What began as a place to help drug addicts soon became a place of forced marriages, forced abortions, and forced sterilizations. In the beginning, I was unaware of anything, except Synanon's assistance to drug addicts. I became his blank canvas. He could do with me as he wished. And he did.

We began our relationship exploring the world of dominant/submissive sex. Somehow this played into the fantasies that had now been stirred up from my childhood sex dreams of being "taken" by a sexy bad boy. For my part, any attention was good. Just as my sister used insanity to be noticed, I used sex. As the submissive in the relationship, I got lots of attention, instructions, and regular orgasms. He was a good lover, and he made sure I was satisfied. He was never physically abusive beyond ordering me around, and if things ever got to a stage where I felt threatened at all, he was more than happy to stop and reassure me until I was relaxed and ready to continue. Our problems didn't stem from our sexual games but rather from his brilliant ability to take information gathered in confidential conversations where we disclosed our deepest and most private secrets and use that information to manipulate, escalate, and create fear and insecurity.

One case in point was a confession I'd made to him that I'd spent most of my life waiting to go insane, like my sister. It had been harrowing to grow up in an environment saturated with the irrationality of insanity. It was made worse by the knowledge that schizophrenia is an inherited disease, and with my having a family filled with mentally ill relatives way out of proportion to the national average, he was enabled to use that fear to manipulate every situation in a way that always pointed to me as emotionally unstable and teetering on the brink of losing my mind. When there was an opportunity, he would harp and harp and push and yell and accuse and call me names until I truly was hysterical, out of control, and yes, very near the brink of breaking down. But as is the case with most abusive people, he waited until after we were married to begin to escalate the abuse. He stopped having sex with me, and if I touched him in any way, he would recoil in disgust.

One day I found myself in the walk-in closet with the door barred from the inside, crying hysterically over and over, "He is insane. I am not insane. He is insane. I am not insane." Eventually, I stopped reacting to him. I figured out he was just egging me on like a cat playing with a mouse. I didn't know when he planned to finish me off, but I had no intention of going quietly into the night. We each had our own private offices in a four-bedroom house. Our offices were treated with respect, and privacy was not violated—that is until I started to suspect that not only was he trying to drive me insane but that he was cheating on me too. I think I was better equipped to deal with the insanity issue than the infidelity issue.

Whenever I walked into his office to talk to him, he would immediately switch his computer screen off. It didn't happen once or twice but over and over again. Finally, I confronted him and asked him what he was doing that was so secretive, and after much tearful denial that there was anything going on and accusations that I didn't trust him, he confessed that he was writing a book and he didn't want anyone to know about it because he was so afraid he would fail one more time. He'd been trying to write the book for years, and he was never able to finish it. Lately, he'd been on a writing binge and that's why he was always closed up in his office, and when I walked in to talk to him, he would close down the page. Although I didn't believe him, I have always taken the high road when someone I care about tells me something. I accept it unless I have hard, cold evidence to the contrary. My opportunity to gather hard, cold evidence was just days away.

We had been fighting for weeks. Everything I said set him off on an abusive tirade, and everything he did set me off into tears of victimhood. We were a mess. He suggested that he take a few days on a trip by himself to think things over. I was so stressed out that the idea of being alone in the house for a week seemed too perfect to believe. I blessed the idea, and he didn't bring it up again, until he mentioned over breakfast one morning that he had obtained his airline ticket. He was going to Florida for a week, and he wanted to reassure me how much he loved me.

"It will all be okay," he promised. "I just have to figure out what's wrong with me, not you." When the time for the trip came and I found myself at home alone, the secrets of his office were just too strong for me to ignore. Yes, I admit that going through all of his computer files was, on the face of it, wrong. But once I started finding all of his e-mails from other women and pictures of all the women he was corresponding with, I didn't feel guilty anymore.

Dear Master,

I am following your instructions and have taken off all of my clothes except my black garter belt and black silk stockings with my vibrating dildo in my wet pussy imagining you standing near me watching me. I will not allow myself to climax until you give me permission. I am your slave in every way and will only feel the pleasure you allow me.

Yours always,

Sally

Discovering the AOL saved e-mails in a document folder labeled, of all things, "Finances," was like hitting a pure vein of gold. Had it not been that the content was so disturbing, I would have felt pride in my sleuthing abilities. I now started opening every e-mail in the file, of which there were hundreds, and discovered each one was worse than the last.

Sally,

I will telephone you when it's convenient for me. Do not cum. You must sit there and feel the vibrator and plead for relief, and you are forbidden to cum. When I phone, I will tell you when to orgasm.

Master

My dear Master,

I am so hot and so wet and so on fire. I beg you, please let me cum. Please. I can't stand it much longer.

Sally

My dear slave,

I do not wish to speak with you right now, but because I am a benevolent master, you may now cum. But first, I want you to fill your fingers with your pussy juices and spread them on your face and mouth and finally lick the juices from your fingers and then and only then you may let yourself shoot your cum.

Master

After checking out all of his pictures and finding one labeled Sally, I moved on to the rest of the e-mails. They were endless and all similar. This is the best one, which to this day I can't believe he was careless enough to leave behind.

My Darling,

I appreciated your reminder to erase everything off of my computer. The article by Ann Landers talking about how people get caught because they are too stupid to delete the incriminating evidence from their computers really hit home. I had been saving everything we've shared, not wanting to lose even one word. But you're so right; I need to get rid of everything. If my husband were to discover any of our e-mails, my life as I know it would be over. I am too dependent on him financially to take any chances of losing my rights. By the way, the plans are still on for your visit, right? M will be out of town for that week, and we should have no interruptions. I'm so excited to see if we have the same magic in person as we do on the phone and online. I know we can never really be together forever, between your mentally ill wife and my finances, but we can have moments of happiness. I will be counting the days until we can be together.

Love,

Sally

Believe it or not, the only part of the letter that hit me initially was the "mentally ill wife" comment. What the fuck? The rest of the day was a flurry of paper as I printed every e-mail, letter, picture, and note. I began in the living room and progressed throughout the house, covering every inch of every wall. He was expected home the next evening. It had taken me all week to figure out his various passwords and break into his files. Suffice it to say, he wasn't very imaginative about any of his security measures, and in fact, many of the files were just buried but not protected. Finally, I found the file containing a book in progress. There were only three chapters written, so if he'd been working on it as long as he said, he really wasn't much of a prolific writer. In contrast, his ability to write sexy e-mails to his various "subs" proved he was just writing in the wrong genre.

When I heard his key in the door the next evening, I sat quietly in my office waiting for the other shoe to drop. "Honey, I'm ho …" Silence. More silence. Then nothing. I looked up and he was standing in my office doorway holding a few of his e-mails he must have removed from the wall. He got the message, and his face was red and distorted. His reaction was not what I'd expected. He was mad. I had finally found a crack in his armor. I prepared myself for some type of physical assault, wondering if he was going to kill me or worse, torture me. I needn't have worried. He spat some things at me about violating his privacy and that it was my fault that he had to look outside the marriage for fun because I was such a cold bitch, but he still didn't seem to grasp that I knew he had been with another woman in Florida.

"So, how's Sally?" I asked in wide-eyed innocence. And with that, the marriage ended. I must say, once I'm out of a relationship, I'm out. I don't hang on wishing it would get better or thinking I can change anything. When it's over, it's over. And he was a done deal. All that was left was the paperwork. And so husband number three bit the dust.

Honeymoon, airlifted with our hiking party to the top of a mountain to avoid setting off an avalanche on the Milford Trek (the Trek distance was approximately 50 kilometers) in New Zealand

Honeymoon, crossing a suspended bridge on
the Milford Trek, New Zealand

Chapter 7

And Then There Was Don

DIVORCED. WHY DOES that word resonate with failure? After all, nearly 60 percent of all marriages end up that way. I'd like to think of it as a club of the majority. But I've been divorced three times, so maybe that's not a majority movement. I got up and put on a heavy sweatshirt and warmer pants. The beach house was bare and basic, and the heater gave off minimal heat, but it was mine. The house was bought and paid for with my money, and sitting here in November in front of the computer searching various singles sites for an appropriate date in this calming silence felt like I was sitting in a small corner of heaven. It was monotonous, though. There were so many lost souls searching for that perfect mate. Never mind that they were twenty years older than they'd disclosed on their profile. From past experience, I knew most were fifty pounds overweight, unemployed, and uneducated. Everyone wanted all of his or her dreams to come true all in one person, in spite of the fact that the reflection in their mirror didn't usually match those expectations.

I was more of a realist. I'd be happy with three or four attributes of my choosing, but even that was difficult to find among this group of two hundred or so that the computer search said were my potential matches. As I systematically deleted one after another of the e-mail responses to my personal ad, I came across a real hunk. *Damn, way too young,* I half thought to myself and half said to the cats, although they didn't much care. *And he's in Washington. Could it be worse? He's so GU.* That's geographically undesirable, for those of you who are uninitiated in the language of Internet dating. Flippantly I dashed off a response.

Dear Don,

As much as I appreciate your interest, I'm almost fifteen years older than you, and I'm absolutely not interested in a long-distance relationship. But good luck in finding your match.

Pat

The process of responding to all of the waiting e-mail took most of the evening. A glass of wine, a classical CD, and the company of the computer were enough to fill the night and alleviate any sense of loneliness or lack of connection to the world. Oh shit! I had accidentally opened a response with a picture of a naked guy with the biggest dick I'd ever seen. As much as it felt like an insult, it was also a curiosity. I'd done a lot of dating, and having come of age in the sixties and seventies, I certainly had seen my share of dicks (both literally and figuratively), and this was big. *That's quite enough for tonight. I'm calling it a day,* I thought. Just before I hit the logout button, another response came in from Don, the cute young guy I'd just blown off.

Hi Pat,

Before you delete this, I hope you'll hear me out. Yes, I'm younger than you, but I've always dated women older than myself because I find younger women to be dull and self-absorbed or even worse, desperately looking for someone to father children. I don't want kids, and I love intelligence. And although I'm GU at the moment, I'm getting ready to relocate in LA for business. I think that takes care of all of your concerns, so will you at least correspond with me and see if there's any connection between us? I hope I hear back from you soon.

Don

I sat and stared at the picture of this handsome young man and was torn between laughing at the absurdity of it all and the desire to put duct tape over his mouth and just jump his bones. Instead I replied:

Dear Don,

As much as I think my first instincts were sound, I'm sure there's no harm in writing and getting to know each other. We might even become friends. Who knows?

Pat

Time for bed, I thought. *At least there's great material here for a little sexual fantasy. God, he's cute, sexy, and built like a bouncer. What's wrong with this picture?* Red flags were waving in every inch of my psyche, and in the true spirit of universal denial, I was able to ignore each and every one. Hey, everyone has to be good at something, and I have an advanced degree in self-delusion. And with that last thought, a shake of my head, and a roll of my eyes, I turned the computer off, put the space heater on in the bedroom, and got ready for bed.

Walking around the little house, which was built as a summer cottage in the fifties, I felt a sense of pride, independence, and freedom. Maybe being single was better than being married. Maybe this was the beginning of the rest of my life and not just a cliché. Maybe this was happiness. Maybe—but sleep was more compelling than all the possibilities of consciousness. There was sheer joy in just slipping between clean sheets with no demands from a partner, no small talk, just dreams where everything is possible.

The cats jumped up on the bed and pushed against the familiar outline of their beloved master's body. Sundance fell asleep almost before his beautiful head hit the pillow, and his regular breathing and almost inaudible snoring were the comforting opiate that always put me immediately to sleep. Butch, on the other hand, had circled my head, walked across my chest, and then pushed his back up against me as we spooned with a familiarity of an old couple.

At work on Monday, I'd wasted at least three hours writing back and forth with Don. It was beginning to occur to me that this was doable. This could be real. He was so earnest and so sincere and so fucking sexy. We were talking on the phone about four hours every night using a cumbersome Internet connection to save money. We'd shared everything and anything except sex, and somehow, it was even sweeter this way. It was so innocent and so romantic. I just had to see him in the flesh. We both needed to discover if there was something there to be nurtured into something even bigger or if it was just a very exciting fantasy E-Ticket ride. Unfortunately, Don was broke. Everything he owned was tied up in getting his software package done, and all of his energy was focused on finding investors. Thank goodness he hadn't asked me for any money. This would have been a red flag serious enough to send me running. But he only mentioned that there were really cheap tickets on Alaska Airlines that he wished he could afford to buy so he could come down to LA and meet me. For the life of me, I couldn't think of any reason why I shouldn't buy it for him. Hell, I waste more money each year on makeup while I waited in the pharmacy for a prescription to be filled.

That night, while we were talking about our dreams, desires, ambitions, and every other thought that came to mind, I had to throw it out.

"Come visit me. I'll pay. I swear to you that I can afford it."

"No way will I let you do that. When I can afford it, I'll come, but not one minute sooner. I'm not going to take advantage of you. We'll just have to be patient. You know how much I want to meet you. I'm going crazy here with my nutty roommate. She really has to get her act together. I keep fixing her up with really nice guys, and she just shows up dressed like a lumberjack. And then, she barely says a word. What a surprise! They never call her back. I'd give anything to get out of here. Hey, did you ever find someone to help you in your office? I'd be a fantastic administrative assistant."

Bingo. That was it. I desperately need an assistant, and maybe, just maybe, something more could happen here. "Yes, as a matter of fact, I've run out of applicants. I think you'd be perfect. What if I gave you a thirty-day trial? If it doesn't work out, I'll give you a ticket home. I feel like I know you, I like you, and you're smart. I'd say a month of telephone conversations is the longest interview on record. So, will you accept a ticket now?"

I was grinning from ear to ear into the phone. Even if it didn't work out on a personal level, I needed an assistant, and it would be a pleasure to have such a sweet guy working for me. I'd been feeling like the television personality Murphy Brown lately with the long line of incompetent, bizarre souls coming and going in the role of my assistant. "Can I stay with you just until I get settled? I'll get my own place as soon as I can get first and last month and a security deposit together."

Don sounded so excited and sincere that I didn't even see the brick wall just around the corner that my speeding car was sooner or later going to hit. I just joined the excitement and couldn't wait to hang up and call my best friend, Dan, to tell him what was happening.

"You're what? Are you crazy? What could you be thinking?" Dan was less than enthusiastic about my disclosure of this latest potential romance. "Pat, I love you, I admire you, and I think you're beautiful. I think you're wonderful, but I also think you're an idiot when it comes to men. Who is this guy? You're going to let him into your home, your office, into your life without having met him? I'm having you committed. Go to your front door and wait for the ambulance. I want you to get in without fighting. Do you understand?"

I smiled affectionately. Dan was probably right, and I'd probably be sorry somewhere up the road, but right now, this minute, I was going for it. What the hell? Whatever the consequences were, they wouldn't be boring, and at the moment, that sounded just fine.

"Sweetheart, I love you, too. It's a thirty-day trial! I'm just going on an adventure. Don't worry. I need something to take the taste of sick, neurotic husband number three out of my mouth and my mind. I need something to dream about and something to get excited about. It will probably turn out to be a very expensive lay, and so be it. I'm just so ready for some fun."

Dan laughed. It's hard to argue with someone who's so intent on her own destruction. "So, when does he get here?" Dan decided to get the rundown.

"He's arriving on Alaska Airlines tomorrow night at 5:00."

"What? I don't believe you. You are such a slut! You'd better tell me everything." Dan spoke with affection and disbelief.

"I promise. I won't leave out a single thing."

And I meant it. Telling Dan about my adventurers was almost as good as the adventures themselves. As I hung up the phone, I felt almost smug in my good fortune. No matter what happens in my life, I have a circle of friends who love me, worry about me, include me in their lives, and always keep me in their hearts. But sex was something I also needed, and my gay friends just couldn't give me that. It's probably a good thing, too. At least I knew they were friends for life. There would never be any silly fights about inconsequential things that lovers seem to go nuts about. No, that was saved for lovers. If I ever figured out why, I'd be a billionaire. But for the moment, I included myself among the ignorant. Tomorrow couldn't come soon enough as far as I was concerned.

I felt his arms hold me as he entered me with all of the strength and control that I'd prayed for. His powerful arms surrounded me, and he seemed to read my mind. Everything I'd ever wanted from a man, he supplied. Without instruction, and without hesitation, he just did it. I was screaming and clutching onto him so hard that briefly, I was afraid I might hurt him. "Harder, oh my God, don't stop." I was having an orgasm with such force, I thought I might explode. And then, I heard a sound off in the distance. It seemed to be getting closer and closer until I thought it must be right in my ear. Shit, it was the alarm clock. I was alone. It was morning.

As I prepared for work, I kept in mind that I was going to the airport directly from the office and whatever I did this morning was what Don was going to see this evening. I took a slow, steamy shower, and for once I had a good hair day. When I checked my image in the mirror on the way out the door, I was pleased with what I saw. I was trim at fifty and youthful enough to pass for thirty-five. This was going to be fun. The day would drag, but eventually I'd feel his six-foot body while I gazed into his strikingly green eyes. I could still feel his touch from my dream. A little voice in the back of my mind shrieked something about how misleading photographs could be and how people lie about their weight and age. I knew there would be something seriously wrong with him, but I chose to turn up the radio, ignore the voices in my head, and proceed to the office.

The day was excruciatingly long. Everything that could go wrong did. Every client in my accounting practice had an insurmountable problem. Everything was earth shattering, and everything had to be handled that instant. When it was time to leave for the airport, I was still returning client calls on my cell phone as I stepped into the elevator and felt a huge sense of relief when finally the calls stopped as the signal grew weaker as I submerged deeper into the belly of the building and closer to my car. The traffic on the drive to the airport was impossible, but the Burbank Airport itself was a pleasure. *Thank God he didn't land at LAX in the middle of rush hour*, I thought.

There was plenty of parking with only a couple of small terminals and no great difficulty in finding the Alaska Airlines passengers' arrival area. I'd brought a book and plenty of change to get all the junk food I could consume from the vending machines as I nervously waited. My stomach was clenched in the vicinity of my throat. Now while I waited, I thought of all the possible outcomes to this hare-brained idea, and I was somewhat sobered. I didn't know this guy. For all I knew, he was a serial killer just waiting to get inside my house, kill me, and somehow clean out my bank accounts. The cats weren't going to be much of a challenge for him. Dan was right. I'm an idiot.

My worst fears were finally coming true. I had gone insane. As these thoughts were racing through my mind, the passengers from Don's flight began entering the waiting room. I gazed intently at each male to see if he was also looking for me. Finally, a guy got off the plane that had to be him. He was the right size with the right look, but with a big potbelly and no sex appeal. *Oh well, at least he doesn't look dangerous,* I thought. But as I started to walk toward him, an older man ran up and gave him a bear hug and off they went arm in arm. *Oh, thank goodness.* I felt a surge of relief. I really had hoped that wasn't the man who took me in his arms last night in my sleep.

It seemed like hundreds of people deplaned, and still no one even remotely resembled Don. So, all that worry was for nothing. He probably cashed in the ticket and I'd never hear from him again. Oh well, nothing ventured, nothing gained. As I started to gather my things to get the heck out of there, I noticed the last few stragglers walking down the ramp. *Oh my God, look at that piece of work.* He walked up to me, took me in his arms, and kissed me gently on the lips. There was only one thought that went through my mind: *Whatever this is, I'm going for it.*

We were self-conscious and awkward, but it only made me like him more. As we walked toward the car, we made small talk and somehow floated back to my house. We talked for hours, and as the sun came up, we were still talking. It seemed impossible to find so much to share after having talked to each other every night for hours on end for over a month. Finally, we made love, over and over. And then we made love again. Everything worked, and everything felt good. It had been a long time for both of us, and no matter what else was to happen, this was real.

The next day was Saturday, and the weekend stretched deliciously in front of us. It felt as though we'd been together forever, and as is the case for most lovers, nothing would ever be better than this place and this moment. It was this memory that would hold us together when the going got tough. This would be the image that would be our glue, because this was as good as it gets. Don took my car to run some errands and to pick up some things at the market. While he was gone, I called Dan to give him an update.

"Dan, I can't believe it. He's actually better than his picture. We are having so much fun. I think he'll be wonderful in the office. He's got such a wonderful work ethic, and such a happy attitude."

Dan laughed and said, "Forget about the work ethic. There was a huge earthquake felt halfway around the world at about 5:30 last night. Would that have been you?"

We both laughed as I told him about the fireworks and about what a great lover Don was, and when I neglected to stop for breath, Dan just laughed and let me go on and on.

Chapter 8
Remodeling for Dummies

"Hey, that's my job!" Don had the sweetest smile, and he took his responsibilities of taking care of me seriously. He opened my door, he ran my errands, he drove, and he did anything heavy or dirty and protected me from all danger, real or imagined. At the moment, I was struggling to drag a box of books from the library to the hall for Goodwill to pick up. He gently pushed me aside and easily picked up the entire box and carried it to the other side of the house. We had fallen into a comfortable domestic arrangement. Don was a whiz at the office. What a handsome, professional, well-tempered addition he was. Every day I had the pleasure of seeing Don at the breakfast table, of watching him work at his desk just outside my office door, of going to lunch with him, of driving home with him, of eating dinner with him, and of laying on the couch watching television with him and ending some days by making perfect love with him before falling into a blissful slumber.

It all seemed too good to be true. This was not a passing fancy. This might well be the rest of our lives. This was starting to be the beginning of forever. At times I had very dark premonitions that something was wrong. Some feeling or emotion was not right, but so much felt so good that the pieces that didn't fit were easily ignored. It's not unusual to revel in what's good and ignore what's bad. Everyone does it, don't they? If someone were to ask me to list the things that were bad between Don and me, my mind would have been blank. It wasn't anything specific. It was a vague feeling. He needed to sleep in the guest bedroom because he was a very light sleeper and needed total darkness to sleep comfortably. We made love once a week now, never less but never more. It was wonderful, always good, just less often. He was less grateful for the gifts I gave him. In fact, he expected more and more.

When we went to a restaurant for dinner, he ordered the most expensive thing on the menu without a thought But, he was still always good to me, always rushing to help, to do, to take care of me. He suggested that he could put down a new floor in the beach house. It would be wonderful to get rid of the pink carpet that came with the house. He had stopped working at the office because he felt it was detrimental to our relationship. He wasn't comfortable working for me anymore. Maybe remodeling the beach house would save me some money in the long run. The place could use endless fixing up. But he wanted to move out to the beach house while I stayed in the city house and worked. Of course, I'd come out to the beach on the weekends and we'd have time together then.

It made logical sense, but it didn't feel good. I would be in the city working every day and he'd be at the beach house doing whatever. But he seemed so happy, and the new hardwood floor would be beautiful. The first few weeks were a flurry of pulling up carpet, ripping up moldings, and wreaking havoc. I gave Don his own credit card so he could buy materials and got him his own car so he could get around. We were a couple, and each person's work was valuable. Why did it feel so uncomfortable? Each weekend when I got to the beach, it looked like there was more mess and less floor. After several months, the floor began to emerge, but only in a couple of areas. Mostly the house was just filled with debris.

"Hey!" Don brightly greeted me on the phone as I sat at my desk juggling files and loose papers. He asked, "Are you working hard?"

I snapped at him, "I'm buried. What's going on? How's the floor coming?" I knew the answer, but I just couldn't help myself from asking.

"I've got a brilliant idea," he continued. "I'm going to take down the spiral staircase and build a new one against the wall. It will open up the entire house. You won't believe the room it will give you, and the architectural lines will make the house seem huge. I might as well take down the dining room wall, too. It's going to be so beautiful. That's why I've been stalling a little bit on the floor. I've been doing sketches, and I think I finally have it all laid out. It didn't make sense to put the floor down until we were sure that it was going to stay that way. What do you think?" I could imagine Don smiling with great pride on the other end of the phone, but I wasn't feeling all that enthusiastic.

"I'm speechless. I don't know. What about your project? What about your business? How much will the supplies cost? Don, I need to think about this. This is no way to make that kind of a decision. I really hadn't planned on making such a big architectural statement. It's just a little A-frame. Geez, Don. Why are you laying this on me now in the middle of the day with a thousand things going on? Can't this discussion wait until I get home and we can talk it over? I can't give you an answer right now. I've got to go. I've got clients in the waiting room and clients waiting on the phone."

I was rattled. This was getting out of hand. As it was, the house was a shambles. I dreaded going to the beach because it was like going to the city dump. No really, I'm not exaggerating; there was a dumpster in the dining room, the furniture was piled in one corner of the house, and there hadn't been any noticeable change for months. When I arrived each Friday night, Don was usually vegetating on the couch watching television, drinking coke, eating pizza, and pretty much enjoying life. *No way. No more new projects. The floor needs to get finished and then, maybe. We'll see. Maybe Don should move out and get a job and we should explore a separation. Maybe he needs to remember that life isn't a free ride.*

"Hey, don't get worked up." It was as if Don had read my thoughts. He then dropped his bombshell. "I hate to tell you this, but I already tore the wall down. I was sure you'd be thrilled. The staircase is kind of balancing precariously on a rope, and I've rented a blow torch to cut it up into pieces so we can dispose of it. Come on, honey. I promise it will be cool. I promise."

And as usual, I smiled and let him soothe me. And I let him start another project. "Okay, but I'm moving out to the beach full time. I'll commute to the city. This living arrangement, with us each living in separate places has got to stop."

"Great, that's perfect. I kind of have to figure out how to get you up to your room, though. There aren't stairs." We both laughed as co-conspirators. It was going to be all right. We were in this together again. I was excited about the prospect of moving to the beach house. I hated the house in the valley. It was the house I bought with my ex-husband, and I no longer felt any connection to it. The maintenance cost a fortune. Between the pool man, the handyman, the cleaning lady, and the gardener, I felt like I was supporting way more people than I needed to. Maybe I should just sell the valley house, keep the rental property, and live at the beach. Maybe I was just jealous that Don got to do whatever he wanted while I worked myself into an early grave. It seemed like everything in my life was surrounded by doubts.

On the way back to the valley after work, my mind was going a mile a minute. I was so excited that when I got home, I put the cats in the carrier and drove immediately out to the beach house. I wanted to start living there right now. As I pulled up to the house unannounced, Don came running out, scooped me up in his arms, and took me right there in the entry way on the floor at the front door. The debris was okay, the staircase was okay, and the floor in whatever state it was in was okay. We were okay. We were a couple. I called in sick and didn't leave the beach house for four days of giggling, cuddling, and hanging out. It was like it was in the beginning.

On Tuesday, I reluctantly drove back to the city for work. We had decided that I'd bring whatever I would need to live full time at the beach on the coming Saturday, but I'd spend every night at the beach until then. My day was filled with the usual stress and frustrations. When my new secretary buzzed me and told me that a woman was on the line, I took the call absentmindedly. I didn't even think to ask who it was. I just grabbed the phone and parroted my usual announcement. "This is Pat, how can I help you?"

"Hi Pat, my name is Barb, and I'm an ex-girlfriend of Don's. I think you need to know some things about him. I don't think you know who you're with."

I took a deep breath. I had almost made it through the day without any unexpected shocks. Don had told me about Barb, but his version had her as the villain and him as the poor, abused victim. "Okay, what do you need to tell me?" I had on my business hat, and I was rational and analytical. This was about damage control. This was a jilted lover. Whatever she had to say, it was colored by the fact that she was no longer with Don. But it wouldn't hurt to listen. Information was good.

"Did you know that he took me for a lot of money? He was supposed to remodel my trailer, and he got halfway through when he left me high and dry. My parents had to help me finish it. I was his business partner, and he just dumped me. The repairs on the trailer were unfinished, and he never paid me a penny for the work I did for his company. He owes me about ten thousand dollars, and he doesn't take my phone calls. He acts like he never knew me, like he never lived with me. He just cut off all communication and acts like I did something to him."

I listened. My mind was speeding. *Oh shit*, I thought. *I'm in big trouble here. The house is never going to be finished, and when it suits him, he'll just dump me.* I shook my head and decided that there was nothing I could do. "Listen, Barb, you're probably right, and Don and I will probably come to an awful end. But for this moment, things are okay. I'm willing to go with this. I wish I could make things better for you, but I can't. I'll have my own price to pay." Barb started to say something, and then she just hung up.

Not ten minutes later, there was another call from another woman. *What the fuck is this*, I thought? For some reason, I wanted to laugh. I wasn't so far gone that I couldn't see the humor in all this. I was glad at least the sex was good. I answered the phone with my usual salutation. "Hello, this is Pat." Sue was nervous, and her voice was strained as she spoke.

"My name is Sue, and I'm Don's business partner."

"Oh, hi Sue. Don's not working here anymore. He's out at the beach house."

Sue quickly interrupted, "I didn't call to talk to Don. I called to talk to you."

Double shit, I thought. I didn't know what was coming, but I was pretty sure it wasn't going to be pleasant.

"Do you know I've invested over seventy thousand dollars in Don's business? Do you know that he's just shined me on and he's shined on the project? Do you know that he's a pig? Do you know that he'll take you for everything you've got, and then he'll just dump you like you're yesterday's garbage?"

"Actually, you're the second woman to call me in the last ten minutes, so I'd say, yes, I know he's a pig, and I know he'll rip me off for whatever I let him get. I don't plan on letting him get too much, but other than that, we are having a lot of fun. He isn't capable of earning a living, but he is smart, and he can do things that help me. I don't want to minimize your loss, but I'm not letting him get seventy grand."

"Look, Pat. Why don't you just buy me out? You can buy my interest in his company. He seems to listen to you more than anyone he's been with. Maybe he'll finish the project and you'll both make a fortune. I'm just too far away to put pressure on him and get him to produce."

I had to smile at that. Oh yeah! Let me write you a big old check right now. "No, I think I'll let you keep your share of the business, especially since I don't believe he'll ever finish it, let alone sell it. I'm sorry, Sue. Don's not going to accomplish anything anywhere near his potential. It's sad. It's heart breaking. But it isn't going to happen. You know it. I know it. The only difference between us is that I can afford him, and you can't. That's about it."

Sue continued, "How can you stand him? How can you be with him? He's a thief. He uses people."

"Sue, I think he's changing. I think he seriously wants to make things work with me. I need to believe that. It doesn't matter what he's done before, but it does matter what he's doing now. And now, he's working hard on the remodel. He's good to me. He takes care of me. And I support him. That's the deal."

We hung up, and all the confidence that I'd mustered for the phone call melted away. I sat there for the longest time trying to decide what to do. But the reality was that my house was buried in debris and Don was in the middle of putting all the pieces back together. There was a lump in my throat and a cramp in my stomach. "I'm going home, Roberta. I'll see you in the morning."

Roberta glanced up to say good-bye and remarked, "You look like the world just came to an end. Are you okay?"

"Oh, I'm just very tired. See you tomorrow."

I was deep in thought the entire way home. I kept trying to reconcile in my mind the story as told to me by Don and the versions told to me by Barb and Sue. The only similarities were that they each knew and had worked with Don. Other than that it was anyone's guess which more closely resembled the truth. And then, of course, there was the reality that each person's perception is true to them regardless of the facts.

"Hi babe, I'm home." I yelled out my usual greeting.

Don met me at the door with a big smile. He was full of gossip about the day. I listened with feigned interest and when he was done, I asked, "Guess who called me today?" I baited him, watching his expression as he responded.

"Russell Crowe?" He had his most darling grin on his face as he waited for whatever shit was getting ready to hit the fan.

"Sue and Barb both called me today."

"What in the world did they want with you?" Don seemed sincerely surprised. "What do you mean? Did they call together or what?"

I explained, "Oh, they both had tons to say about you and your faults. They both called within ten minutes of each other. Are they friends? Could they have taken turns?" The silence was deafening.

I continued, "They didn't say anything that was too surprising, but it was a little unexpected as to how wronged they both felt. Did you wrong them?"

I gave Don my biggest grin. I wanted him to feel safe. I wanted to see how much he would tell me if I didn't make him feel threatened or cornered. There would be plenty of time for that once the house was finished. Don appeared sincere in his answer. "Sue just can't accept that the company is over. It didn't work out. Her investment is gone. I'm sorry, but what can I do? Anyway, I intend to pay her back every penny. It just won't be on her schedule. It will be when I can. And Barb, well, I guess the best way to describe her problem is that she wanted to be with me, and I didn't want to be with her, and it made working with her very awkward."

I bit my tongue and let it go. There would be nothing to gain by confronting him. He was like a little kid who would never be responsible for anything that happened. It would always be someone else's fault. It wasn't a lie to him. That's how he saw it. It was his truth. It never occurred to him that it was odd that everything always went wrong, and it was never his doing. As I climbed the makeshift stairs to my room, I gave Don a gentle kiss goodnight to let him know that there was no problem, that life hadn't changed. I accepted him as he was, and there was a look of surprise on his face. He had expected a battle.

Chapter 9

When Denial is Not a River in Egypt

SHIT, SHIT, SHIT, shit, shit. Now that denial was a thing of the past, I was confronted with a lot of demons. The house was a disaster, and some of Don's statements were irrational. He wasn't working on his project, and he didn't have a job, but he expected Sue and me to believe he was going to pay her back seventy thousand bucks in this lifetime. He didn't seem to feel bad or guilty or really any responsibility at all. The odds of my house getting finished were just about zero, and the debris and trash were very literally a health risk. How did I approach it? My stomach was in knots all the time now. My head throbbed, and my entire body was clenched tight. Work was a nightmare of stress and deadlines without all of this. Sex on the entryway floor wasn't going to cut it. All night, I dreamed of trash, debris, and unfinished repairs. I had to motivate Don to get the work done so that I could throw him out. The throwing out part was pretty much a given at this point, but no one was going to be able to come in and finish the work he started without charging me a fortune. Finally, morning came, and I dragged myself downstairs to face Don and talk to him. I knew I had to stay rational, as he would not deal well with hysteria. Of this I was sure.

As usual, he was still sleeping soundly. He slept late every morning and went to bed early every night. I was lucky if I saw him two or three hours by the time I commuted the hundred and ten miles of my daily round trip. I wondered how I was going to get him up so we could talk. I knew he'd be grumpy if I woke him. I decided there was only one thing that would work. Out in the yard, I gave the trash can a few very loud bangs right outside Don's bedroom window. Then, just as quickly, I ducked back into the garage and back into the house just in time to find Don racing out of his bedroom, half in and half out of his jeans, ready to kill someone.

"What's wrong, Don?" I was all innocence.

"What the fuck was that? Who's out there? I'm going to kill someone!"

I went into the kitchen and waited for whatever would pass, but at least Don was wide awake, and when he got back from checking out the perimeter of the house, I'd have coffee waiting for him, and he'd be mine. Let the conversation begin.

"I couldn't find anyone. Who was that? God, I was sound asleep and I just about jumped out of my skin."

Don was whining as though I should feel sorry that he had to wake up. With great difficulty, I acted sympathetic. "Hon, sit down and have some fresh coffee. It's already brewing. I have a few minutes before I have to leave for work."

I was hoping he wasn't going to connect the dots, but he was too sleepy to be anything but focused on his missed sleep. "So, what's on the agenda for today? Do you have all the supplies you need?"

Don looked at me like I was speaking a foreign language. His biggest plans for the day probably included sleeping, reading, and watching movies. "I don't know. I guess I'll work on the staircase. I'm still designing it, though. I haven't got all the bugs worked out. Once I get it drawn, actually building it won't take any time at all."

We both knew that was a lie, but what could I say? If I called him a liar, we'd be off and running into a fight, and the outcome would be controlled by emotions, and that's the last thing I wanted. I already knew of two cases that proved emotions don't turn out well for anyone but Don. "Would it be a problem to focus on getting the debris out of the house? I'd really appreciate it, and I think it would make things more comfortable for both of us. What do you think?" My voice was calm, loving, and without fight. I gave him a quick peck on the lips and left. I didn't feel any better, but at least maybe some trash would be missing when I got home. If I had to live this way much longer, I would have a nervous breakdown. I could feel my organized and well-planned life slipping further and further out of my control, and I didn't like the feeling at all.

As I drove home along Pacific Coast Highway the fifty-odd miles to the beach in Oxnard, my hands were clenched on the steering wheel, and I was talking to myself. The conversation revolved around the fact that I was certain that nothing was going to be different than when I walked out the door this morning. Finally, I pulled off to the side of the road, turned the radio up, and cried. There was no specific reason, just a release of pent-up nerves and frustration. After a few minutes, I felt almost refreshed. My reflection in the mirror looked worse that I felt, so I took a few more minutes to freshen up so that by the time I arrived home, I'd look just like I did when I left this morning.

"Hey Don, I'm home."

Don looked up from the couch with a shit-eating grin on his face. "Hey babe, you look tired. Let me get you something to eat. Come on. Sit down, take off your shoes, and let me take care of you. It must have been a bad day. You look pale and tired and just out of it."

I looked around and felt that I was in a strange room. "Something's different. Oh my God! I can see the floor. Oh, honey. Thank you. Thank you. Wow, you put in a good day's work, didn't you?"

I could see that he had, in fact, done quite a bit of work. Maybe he was going to actually get something done. It was too much to hope for, but all I could do was continue positive reinforcement and hope he would continue. "What would you like for dinner?" he asked as he continued to massage my feet and generally soothe me. "I have chicken defrosting, and there's plenty of stuff for a salad in the fridge. Here, let me get you a glass of wine while I go putter in the kitchen." Don served me dinner with gentleness and generosity. He listened to me talk about my day and said all the right things at all the right places. After dinner, he took me in his arms and made perfect love to me. It felt good. Of course, it didn't mean anything in the whole scheme of things, but it felt good, and for this minute, that was enough.

Just before I went upstairs to bed, I remembered that I was a bit cold the previous night, so I went into the garage to look for an electric space heater. When I opened the back door and put the light on in the garage, I almost threw up. All of the debris from the house had been tossed carelessly into the garage. It looked like a landfill, but this was my garage. I should have realized that it was too good to be true, but this was so much worse than I'd expected that the sobs wouldn't stop. I just stood there and howled. There was no more rational Pat. There was no more understanding Pat. In fact, I wasn't even mad. I was way beyond mad. I was only moments away from rage. Don came running out, and he understood immediately what was happening. He took me in his arms and promised that he'd get a dumpster delivered and get all the trash cleared out of the garage by the end of the week. He poured more wine until I stopped sobbing, and the whole time he stroked me and made promises and told me he was going to work harder and get stuff done faster, and he told me that I had to trust him. It was going to be okay. Honest. So he said. Between the wine, the food, the sex, and the emotions, I slept the dreamless sleep of the dead. I didn't toss, and I didn't wake up until morning. Even then, I just dressed and left. I was almost relieved that Don was still sleeping. I had nothing to say. I was ready to throw him out. It didn't matter anymore what shape the house was in. It was over.

Chapter 10

The More Things Change,
the More They Stay the Same

SEASONS COME AND seasons go, and even the worst remodeling project does come to an end, eventually. I looked around the beach house and realized that two years did make a difference. The house was finished. It was even beautiful. With the wall that separated the living room and the dining room gone, the vaulted ceiling had a cathedral look. The open kitchen and newly painted cabinets were clean and modern looking. And reluctantly I had to admit that the new fireplace was pretty spectacular. The new staircase that hugged the wall did in fact make the house appear huge, just as Don had promised. Not that the cost had been cheap, though. Don and I were barely speaking to each other, and every day Don demanded more and more things. We had settled into a routine that was profoundly predictable, and on some level, I got more satisfaction from that than any other bizarre fact of our life together. Don was a really strange bird.

We took a trip to China when American Express offered two round-trip business class tickets for twenty-five hundred dollars. The trip had been memorable in that I decided to retire after spending a month cruising up the Yangzi River with ten other couples. I observed how old and tired and used up the men all looked. I could see myself in ten or fifteen years completely stressed out and ready for a hospital gurney. I was already taking close to fifteen prescription drugs for every conceivable stress-related disease. What in God's name would I be taking in fifteen years if I didn't make some major changes in my life soon? On my first day back to work, I made a phone call to an old colleague offering to sell him my accounting practice. He said yes, and

I was ready to start a new life. And it was time to find out if that was going to be a life with or without Don. I'd been on the fence for so long, poised to throw him out almost daily and pulling back for one reason or another.

Don had been researching the purchase of a motor home. I was so unenthusiastic, I almost was unaware of the whole process until finally one afternoon he told me we needed to take a drive, as he had something to show me. We drove for a couple of hours, and we both settled into our own thoughts and daydreams until we came to a stop at a used RV dealer. The lot was filled with old trailers and motor homes. I looked over at Don, and he was beaming like a cat dropping a dead rat at his master's feet. I would have preferred the dead rat. "Come on! You won't believe the deal I found," Don purred.

"Can I help you folks?" The sleazy salesman eagerly interrupted us when he walked up, quite excited to have a prospective customer.

Don stepped forward. "Hi, I called you this morning. You have a twenty-four foot 1984 Bounder motor home for sale?"

The salesman's face lit up with pleasure. "Oh boy, are you in luck. I've had people looking at that motor home all morning, and the last one said they would come back this afternoon with a decision. So far, they're a no show. You've got to see it; I know you'll be impressed. We can't keep these things in stock. They come in on trade-ins and then they go out within a day or two. We've just had this since yesterday, and we haven't had a chance to clean it up yet."

We followed him to a very large, very old motor home. Having never seen one up close before, and certainly having never entered one, it was not at all what I, or Don for that matter, expected. It was amazing; an entire home on wheels for ten grand. Even if it was a monstrous mistake, that was not a lot of money for an adventure of this proportion. The salesman went away and left us alone to explore, talk, dream, and plan the possibilities of escaping in this gargantuan, for lack of a better word, thing.

"I'm speechless," I blurted out. "It's amazing. Can you imagine traveling in this?"

I was giggling for the first time in months. It had been awhile since we'd been this giddy. Don was very proud of himself. He took control and explained to me what we needed to do. Don negotiated everything since we'd been together. I was embarrassed to negotiate. I felt if the asking price was reasonable, it was easier to just pay it. "I'll offer him nine grand, but it's worth at least eleven, so that gives us a lot of room to negotiate. I'll be the bad cop and you be the good cop. But, whatever happens, follow my lead."

I smiled. This was the Don I adored. It was such a pleasure to have him take charge. It didn't even matter if it was something I wanted or not. I just liked being taken care of. This was why I hadn't thrown him out. This was why

I put up with all of his neurotic behavior, which on a good day was endless. "Okay, boss. Where you lead, I will follow." And I meant it sincerely and from the bottom of my heart.

The negotiations were typical of any used vehicle purchase. We haggled. We walked out. The salesman chased after us. The price went up and the price went down, and within two hours, we were the proud owners of an old Bounder motor home. As Don drove away, and I followed in the car, we both had grins on our faces way out of proportion to what had just transpired. The drive home was hysterical. Don was scared to change lanes, and I was instructed to move over and block his lane whenever he put the turn signal on, and I did so with great concentration. Team work was fun. The motor home swayed and swerved and bounced all over the road, and I hoped this was normal, but it sure didn't look like it. Somehow we managed to get back home safely and parked the RV in front of the house. The lot was forty feet wide, and the twenty-four-foot RV filled the street. Geez, it looked even bigger than it did on the dealer's lot, and from the second floor, it was still visible. *So*, I thought, *where to now?*

The next couple of weeks were a whirlwind of repairs, maintenance, and preparation for our maiden voyage. Most of it was over my head, but Don was the happiest I'd seen him in a long time. And when the day came that we were ready to take off, we were both filled with anticipation and excitement. Loading the RV was easy. We packed everything. We were planning a three-week trip to give us a chance to see what this was all about. As usual, Don had researched everything, planned the route, and even went so far as to choose which RV parks we were going to stay at. All I had to do was write the checks and do the cooking and cleaning. That was a laugh, since I hadn't cleaned or cooked in almost twenty years. Don was in for a real surprise, but maybe he'd lose a little of that excess weight he'd been putting on since we'd hooked up. Or maybe I would rise to the occasion, and my old Stepford wife cooking skills would surface. One could only hope.

The one challenge that had been overlooked by both of us was what to do about the two cats. What if they didn't adjust to this new means of transportation? Would it be three weeks of screaming and hissing, or would there be peace and contentment? There was no way to find out, except to pack them in and start the trip. Of course, it would have been smart to take a trial trip to the next town and back, but that would have required some planning and so far, at least from my perspective, it had been spontaneous from the get go, and this wasn't going to be any different. As we pulled away from the curb, Butch jumped on my lap, stared straight into my eyes, and howled. Sundance huddled under the couch trembling, and Don and I looked at each other, wondering how long three weeks could be if the howling continued.

The rattling of every pot and pan made conversation impossible. But that didn't seem to matter, because for some reason we were both happy with our own thoughts.

This is about as cool as it gets, I thought. Why? There was no rational explanation. Every person we knew thought we'd both lost our minds. Why would I sell a lucrative accounting practice to go off in an old dilapidated RV with a man who tested my composure on a good day? And maybe they were right. But right or wrong, we were committed. We had pointed our skis downhill, and we had pushed off.

Chapter 11
On the Road

As we pulled into the first trailer park, I was spellbound. I'm a city girl, and if you put three trees together, I call it a forest. But this was the most peaceful place on earth. We were in a magical forest with a wide, glistening stream flowing along one edge of the park. Don went in and registered while I administered to the cats. It had been a long and exhausting day. Butch was hoarse from yowling, and Sundance was hunkered down even deeper beneath the couch. No one had given an inch. Butch had an air of anger and disbelief that was really funny when during those few moments of silence it was possible to hear oneself think. The look on his face was of utter disbelief that no one was responding to his demands. He truly was not having any of this. Uh-uh, no way. Butch stopped long enough to realize that something was happening. We weren't moving. He used the opportunity to eat some food from his dish and then, turning his back to me, took advantage of the nearby litter box. Sundance also seemed encouraged by the lack of movement. He stuck his nose out, came over, and rubbed his mouth and head against my knee and let out a little squeak of relief.

I didn't realize the magnitude of Don's planning until we were safely parked in our overnight site. The stream, less than ten feet away, was shimmering in the windshield. We were surrounded by mature trees and little wild things scurrying noisily around the mounds of dead leaves and fallen limbs at the foot of the trees. Butch and Sundance were endlessly entertained by all of the sounds and smells. It was the antithesis to where I had come from. What a relief to be out from under the weight of deadlines, employee demands, client needs, and even social obligations, though many were wonderful and fun, but still an obligation. Also, there was a sense of returning to real life. Working as a CPA with wealthy clients has an emotionally numbing effect. The world starts to look normal at the top and somehow less valuable at the bottom. In reality, there's a lot more people living outside the gilded world of the upper and upper middle class.

In the morning, Don rented a canoe, I packed a lunch, and we glided along the stream taking in the beauty, barely needing to exchange words. Silently, Don pointed out a huge bird very high on a passing branch that looked like a bald eagle. Not really knowing enough about eagles to know for sure, neither one of us cared. It was a big, beautiful bird. Each day on the road was better than the last. Each park was a jewel. The views, the wildlife, the hiking, the friendly neighbors, and the lack of pressure really did have an effect on both of us. I had much more realistic expectations of Don since he obviously couldn't work at a job while we were on the road. I wasn't pressuring him to job hunt, and since he had the pressure off to contribute money to our life, he was able to just do the things he enjoyed and seemed remarkably happy.

The days were uneventful, and the cats remained calm. Cooking and domestic chores were a pleasure. Each day passed in much the same way, except now on the road, the cats slept quietly and pleasantly and only woke up upon arrival. They were already completely adapted to our new life on the road. The trailer parks were magnificent, each one better than the last. If there were any problems at all, it was from the old, dilapidated motor home. The windows leaked when it rained. There was no heat except directly over the heat vents and even then, it was barely warm enough to be comfortable in the chill of night. But that's what blankets and sweaters are for. As for the leaky windows, that's what towels and rags are for. There were few luxuries in the motor home, and it had zero stability on the road. Passing trucks caused the coach to quiver in its lane, and on occasion, the intense wind from an oncoming truck was enough to make it feel like the coach had actually been blown into the next lane.

When we arrived in Cobourg, Oregon, Don didn't go to an RV park but went directly to an RV dealer. I was still asleep in the back of the coach when Don came and got me. "Come on, sleepy head, there's something I want to show you." I stepped out of the motor home and found myself in a dealership lot with enough motor homes to fill an entire city block. There stood row after row of new and used motor homes of all sizes, styles, and makes. "I saw an ad for a wide–bodied, beautiful luxury coach. It sounds awesome. Let's just take a look at it." I was as taken back as Don was enthusiastic.

I was still in the sweats I'd slept in, having not even brushed my teeth, when I found myself sitting opposite an RV salesman talking about what my RV needs were. My mind was racing trying to figure out what Don was trying to create here. Our relationship was much improved these last six months. While tying the loose ends on the sale of the accounting practice, and making plans for the trip, we had pulled together and worked as a team. Things weren't ideal. Don kept emotionally distant, asked for whatever he could get away with, and contributed just enough to be useful, but never more than what was absolutely the minimum requirement. On the road, Don's only responsibilities were to run errands on the bicycle, drive the motor home, and do any mechanical repairs that he could do without causing more problems than solutions. It turned out that his mechanical skills were minimal. Although sex remained fantastic, it was still a once a week thing, and you could tell time by it. It was regular, predictable, and good.

"Let me show you one of our best deals right now," the salesman offered. When I stepped inside the first coach he showed us, my breath was taken away. Never had I imagined anything could be so beautiful, especially after three weeks in the old Bounder. This was an Oregon built Safari Continental wide-bodied luxury coach. It was decked out with a dishwasher, a washer/dryer, televisions in the living room and bedroom, and it was huge. It was thirty-eight feet long and 102 inches wide, the widest body allowed by law. While I walked around the coach, eyes glazed over, my head filled with imagery and fantasies about life on the road in this mega-monster. The salesman was murmuring in my ear about how no cash needed to cross hands. They would write the deal so that the trade-in took care of the down payment and the value was bumped up to allow 100 percent financing. The amount financed would be a scary one hundred thousand dollars, but for this coach, that was a steal. It was a 1995 model still under extended warranty, with only seventy-five thousand miles on it. Diesel engines were expected to go a million miles or more, so for all intents and purposes, this was new. With the warranty, there would be no repair surprises—or so I thought in my naïve world. With all of my street smarts and book learning, I really did live in a virtual bubble of ignorance.

"Don, swear to God this is what you really want to do? I can't handle this thing on my own. You're either in or out. Buying this would be life altering. Are you sure? Is this the life you want to live? What about your projects, your work, what you want to do?" I couldn't believe that I was so tempted to do this.

"I can do it all from the road. Don't worry, this will be amazing. I'll do everything that's dirty and heavy. I'll help you with the chores, and I'll take care of you." Don was without guile and speaking from the heart.

The salesman explained that there was one glitch. In order to be exempt from California sales tax, we had to keep the coach out of California for ninety days. *Frankly,* I thought, *that doesn't seem like much of a hardship. I can't think of anything I'd rather do than actually start traveling.* Of course, when we left California we had intended to be on the road for three weeks. This would mean we couldn't go home, and that was not possible. I decided that I'd leave Don with the problem of moving all of the stuff out of the Bounder into the new motor home and I'd fly back home to take care of money transfers, find a mail forwarding service, and generally shut down the houses for our absence. After some minor discussion, I signed on the dotted line, looked one more time at my new home, and left for a quick trip home to Oxnard Shores.

Arriving at the beach house, the silence was deafening. No cats to listen to my ideas. There was no Don to wait on me, dote on me, and in his own way fill a huge void in me. Being alone was awful. This was the first time in a long time that I realized I was really deeply involved in building a life with Don. We'd been together for over three years and survived the stress of remodeling and the stress of my being the only one contributing money to our lifestyle, and yet we still walked hand in hand, giggled over our silly inside jokes, and talked easily and endlessly about everything and nothing, and as emotionally distant as Don was, I was beginning to believe that this was just who he was. It was a daily struggle deciding if this was enough.

I quickly pulled the finances together and made sure all of our needs would be provided for while we were away. Within two days, arrangements had been made for monthly wire transfers, mail forwarding, prescription forwarding, and most importantly, phone calls to my closest friends to update them on this latest adventure. My friends supported me every step of the way, regardless of what I did. Maybe that was why it was so easy for me to jump from adventure to adventure without really feeling too frightened. No matter what, there were friends to cheer me on. As I pulled the door behind me and prepared to step into the airport shuttle waiting at the curb, I looked back over my shoulder at the charming A-frame that was to be my retirement home. *Not yet,* I thought. *Not just yet.*

Chapter 12
More Change, More of the Same

"WHAT IN THE hell have you done since I've been gone?" I was just inches from falling over the emotional precipice that seemed to be the ongoing state of this relationship. I'd been transferring funds, selling stock, and making huge changes in my financial situation so that we would have a fantastic ninety days on the road. At this point, anything longer than that was going to take a more long-term strategic plan.

"Hey, aren't you going to say hello first?" Don flashed his usual boyish grin, came over, and gave me a kiss and asked how my trip was. Then he added, "I've been making something for you. I bought a used sewing machine with the money you left for emergencies and I made these cool covers for the new couches so the cats wouldn't funk them up. Here, I made curtains for the bedroom windows to keep the light out."

"Have you moved anything from the Bounder to the Safari?" I wasn't that easily distracted. I didn't care if he'd built a shopping center out of a toothpick and a paper clip. I still could see that we had tons of work to do. And how much did the sewing machine and the material cost? All this crap could be bought for a few dollars. Why did he have to be so penny-wise and dollar foolish? Don brought me back from my mental rant.

"Not yet, we can start first thing in the morning. I already talked to our salesman, and he said it wasn't a problem. We can take our time, and if we're done in a few days, that will be soon enough. Don't worry. I made sure everything was okay."

I allowed myself to relax in his arms. It was times like this I had to remind myself how young he was. He didn't have a great sense of priorities or understand how his actions could be perceived differently than intended by others. He lacked the clarity of vision that comes with experience. He was euphoric as he explained, "I've been marking the maps for our route. We can spend the next ninety days going all the way to Key West then come back across the northern states to Washington, and then south to LA. What do you think? "

I smiled. What else could I do? My very own master planner was at work. Why not go with the flow? We were going to go where he wanted regardless of whether I thought it was a good idea or not, and frankly, it sounded like a hoot. Key West here we come. "Okay, come here and make me feel like you missed me," I whispered as Don responded by stepping forward, taking me in his arms, and leading me back to the bedroom.

The next few days passed loading one rig with everything from the other, planning the trip, discussing routes, and picking RV parks based on *Trailer Life Magazine* ratings. Reservations had to be made weeks in advance for some of the more exclusive parks, particularly in Key West, and in some of the more highly rated parks. Finally, everything was done, the route had been chosen, and all that was left was pulling out and hitting the road. Butch and Sundance were comfortably asleep, and as always, they slept end to end in a V formation. Being littermates, they had a strong connection to each other. I never separated them, and the fact that they had both adjusted to this new lifestyle was a huge load off my mind. They were my best buddies. It seemed like the preparation for our departure took forever, but before we knew it, we were on our way, committed to do this as a team (couple?). The fine distinction was always the elephant in the room. To Don, it was a team, and to me, it was a couple. I was able to convince myself that it was the same. Since we didn't have a car, there was nothing to hook up, and as Don slipped behind the wheel, he started barking instructions to me. It was as though every resentment, perceived or real, and every inequity he'd ever felt in life was going to be acted out here and now. He was the one in power now. The look on his face was a little frightening. I had made an expensive commitment, and Don knew I wouldn't causally walk away from it.

"Sit back!" he barked. "Tell me when it's clear, move the mirror in." And so the new Don emerged, and the game of how to not get Don angry began. The ninety days soon passed, and we continued our life on the road. I learned how to manage our finances online, and going home became unnecessary. The next nine months were spent in a choreographed dance between Don controlling every move I made and then bitterly criticizing what I had just done at his request. It was a never-ending spiral that anyone who's ever been abused will recognize. In spite of the manic depressive nature of our sparring with each other, I never lost sight of the fact that I still cared about him. When he was good, he was very, very good, and when he was bad, he was awful.

But there were good times. There were still spontaneous, fun, and affectionate times between us. They were just more and more infrequent.

"Happy birthday, Pat," Don said as he bent down to give me a birthday kiss. I was still asleep in bed when Don rode his bike to buy me a birthday card and a gift with my credit card. I wished I didn't still feel that way, but it really was my credit card, and I really did pay all the bills. And I was starting to resent it again. We'd been on the road for about a year. Most of it was exciting. Watching the space shuttle take off at Kennedy Space Center was a once-in–a-lifetime event. A Key West waterfront site with a private tiki hut, private wharf, and landscaped for privacy in a double-wide space was luxury in paradise. That was a very good month, indeed. So besides the fact that he didn't really care about me, why wasn't all that good stuff enough?

"Thanks, Don." As I opened the birthday card, my eyes quickly scanned to the bottom to see the salutation he chose. His customary line was, "Thinking of you." He never wrote, "I love you," or any other intimate words of endearment. There it was, just as clear as day, at the bottom of the birthday card, the proverbial, "Thinking of you." That's how it ended. At that moment, there was no more Pat and Don. There was only the slow process of ending it.

"Don, do you love me?" It was the question that had been burning on the tip of my tongue for three years. I knew the answer, and I was finally ready to hear it.

"No, Patty. I love my mom. I loved my ex-wife. I loved my grandfather, and by the way, he didn't tell my grandmother he loved her until he was in the hospital just before he died. Love doesn't happen overnight."

I sat back and took a deep breath. "What are your feelings toward me, Don?" I asked, more to document the decision I'd already made than because it would change my mind.

"I like you a lot. I think you're great. I'm happy with you most of the time. But sometimes I get tired of you controlling everything. I need my own allowance. I need my own car. I need my own life."

Yes, it hurt, but more importantly, it finally put the truth on the table. I was now able to make an informed decision. Could I spend the rest of my life supporting a dysfunctional, demanding, selfish child who had little or no feelings for me? Or was it time to cut my losses?

"Honestly, Don, it's not enough for me. I'm done. You can have all those things without me. When we get back to Oxnard, I'll give you the sailboat so you have someplace to live. I'll give you a couple thousand dollars so you have food and dock fees for a couple of months, and you can keep the Jeep to get around in until you can buy something newer and better. But you're on your own. I can't imagine what I'm going to do with this coach without you, but I'd rather be alone than in a loveless relationship with you."

Nothing changed at all between us for the rest of the trip. Don was still critical and controlling. We still made love, or should I say we still had sex once a week. We still checked out all the tourist attractions, and we still did our respective chores and duties. But the elephant was no longer in the room. We were friends with benefits. On the way back to California, Don started teaching me how to take care of the rig. Everything was heavy, manual, and difficult for me to handle. Don was a six-foot, 200-pound, muscle-bound forty-year-old and I was, in a word, not.

It became apparent early on that I would never physically be able to handle the current coach on my own. When we reached Oregon, we stopped back at the dealership where I'd purchased the Safari Continental to take a look at some new models that might be easier for me to handle. When we were presented with a 1998 forty-foot Beaver Patriot with a rock star paint job, endless upgrades, and more bells and whistles than I could have imagined, I needed to make a life-changing decision. Did I really want to do this on my own? I was again offered a deal that was hard to refuse. No money down, just trade in the Safari for the Patriot and start making new payments. The newer coach was twice as much, but the payments were spread over twenty years instead of seven so that my monthly payments actually went down. Somewhere in the excitement of buying the newer coach, the reality of life on the road got lost. I didn't even consider everything that I'd need to do to pull this off. Once again, the task of transferring everything from one coach to the other took my mind off what I'd just done. The learning of how to operate all of the new systems was now totally up to me. My mind was on overload as we finally pulled out of the Cobourg lot and started south to Oxnard.

Don drove, as I sat quietly in the passenger seat. The realization that I would be driving this bus on my own had my heart thumping. For once, I was able to ignore Don's orders and rantings as he drove down the road and focus solely on my own needs and desires. Life was soon to change dramatically, and I was beginning to think it might be a good thing. "Don, I'm selling the beach house. I'm selling the Encino house. I'm getting rid of everything and starting over." Don shrugged as if to say, what's it got to do with me?

Dan visiting Don and I in Key West

Don and I dancing in Key West

Hiking in the Grand Canyon with Don

Caught in a snowstorm somewhere on the road
traveling with Don in the Safari Continental

Chapter 13
Fears and Tears Leaving Oxnard

THE IRONY WAS that I'd spent my professional accounting career relentlessly judging those who didn't meet their deadlines. My clients had compelling reasons to want to avoid them. Each year deaths, family catastrophes, divorce, infidelities, and betrayals frequently dumped the tax preparation on the partner or spouse who had never before handled their finances. Abandoned to organize and summarize the year's transactions, they were paralyzed with fear, indecision, and confusion. How quickly I judged those who came to my office with their eyes glazed over by the overwhelming thought of facing all those random pieces of paper. Their memories were now broken down to entries in a checkbook and statements from a credit card company. Each item was a cruel reminder of what had been and what would be no more. As deadline after deadline passed, I judged them as lazy, stupid, and inferior. I gave help only at a very high fee. And even then, I resented their weakness.

And now I watched as my possessions were being reduced into four piles. I sat cross-legged, staring vacantly at my two friends as they forced me to choose, item by item, four possibilities: trash, charity, storage, motor home. These were my choices. I'd spent seventeen years in a self-absorbed, consumption-driven yuppie existence. I had accumulated real estate, endless mementos from endless trips to endless countries, and volumes of things. My real estate agent and my next-door neighbor had come over early on the day escrow was to close on my last piece of property, my prized beach house. I had parked the motor home in front of the house. I had spent the last thirty days hiding inside its protective walls as I watched television, day after day, ignoring the need to empty the house by 5:00 p.m. this very day. Each time my real estate agent called to check on my progress, I'd report that all was under control and there was no problem in meeting this dreaded deadline.

Now, I was the one who was glazed over, overwhelmed, and unable to function. But my friends treated me as though my lapse was something that warranted love, kindness, and support. Most of all, they treated me without judgment. I felt such sadness for each person I had dismissed as lazy. This wasn't about being lazy. It was about being unable to face real and profound pain.

How I arrived at this dismal state of affairs wasn't really very original, was it? Don and I had planned to sail off into the sunset. I sold my business, bought all the appropriate toys to make a stylish getaway, and then after three years of daily emotional struggle, I ended the relationship. The prospect of continuing alone with a plan that was meant to be our happily ever after was unfathomable. What in God's name was I doing? Did I really believe that I could handle this forty-foot behemoth on my own?

In my heart, I only cared about one thing. I would show him that I could do anything and his absence meant nothing to me. This had been his dream that I supported because it made him smile, and oh how I still loved his smile. Now I pretended it was my dream. But, what I really had was a twenty-year mortgage and pride that didn't allow me to consider any other alternative but to carry on. I'd never driven it. I'd never maintained it. I'd never emptied the holding tanks or filled the fuel tank. At 5:00 p.m. we locked the door of my beach house as escrow officially closed. I felt like Robert Redford when he turned to Paul Newman in *Butch Cassidy and the Sundance Kid*, as they sat perched on the edge of a cliff with the *federales* hot on their tail. Redford said, "But I can't swim!" with Newman responding, "Hell, the fall will probably kill you." And then they both proceeded to jump a trillion feet into a river. That's what it felt like to me.

Toni and Cathy stood at the curb and waved as I pulled away. I was holding the wheel so tightly that my fingers were cramped and locked into position. My destination was Malibu, fifty-five miles away, with my route taking me along the California Pacific Coast Highway. It was a valiant trip, covering a meager distance. As the road curved, climbed, narrowed, and fell, my body was drenched with sweat, and my hands shook. It was difficult enough on the coastal curves built into the cliffs of the Santa Monica mountains, but once I pulled into Malibu, the road got really crowded. This part of PCH is notorious for mudslides, preventative construction, and repairs. The cement barriers are of little concern when zipping along in a car. But if you happen to be in a wide-bodied bus with surfers darting out from between parked cars, not to mention the parked cars themselves, the word crowded takes on a whole new meaning. Although I had driven the entire route in my car the previous day, I wasn't confident that I would be able to get into the left lane when I needed to, assuming, of course, that I didn't hit a parked car or cement barrier before I got there. But luck was on my side. I used my turn signal, checked my mirrors, held my breath, and changed lanes. There was no sound of brakes screeching and no horns. I made it. I had safely arrived at the entrance of the Malibu RV Park.

The coach handled the steep incline into the park easily. I was relieved because I'd been having nightmares about it. I had dreamed that the motor home never reached the top. It felt good to stop, and along with relief came total exhaustion. I'd been so intense and so freaked out for the entire drive that now I barely had the strength to walk into the office to register. My face was red hot, and I was perspiring profusely. My hair was matted with sweat, and my hands were trembling.

I staggered out into the day and stumbled to the registration desk. A truly concerned clerk ran around the desk, put his arm around my waist to steady me, and asked, "Should I call 911? Are you having a stroke?" I laughed and assured him that I was okay. "I just need a minute to regroup. This is my virgin voyage in that thing." I pointed out the window to the motor home, and everyone within the sound of my voice became silent and dumbfounded. They were all thinking what the clerk asked. "But you're so tiny! Where's your husband?" This was the first time I'd been asked to define my status by strangers. I felt like bait in a trap. I'd been warned by everyone I talked to before I'd left Oxnard to always say I'm with someone so that people wouldn't take advantage of me. I was pretty paranoid at this point, but the truth just came pouring out anyway. "It's just me and my two cats."

The clerk was eyeing me suspiciously when he said, "Do you work out of your coach? You look awfully young to be retired."

I shot back, "I look awfully young because I am retired!" And then I laughed and everyone at the desk gave me lots of strokes for having the courage to travel alone in that large but beautiful coach. We proceeded with registration, and when it came time for me to sign, my hands were still shaking so badly that I had trouble holding the pen and even more trouble actually writing my name.

Once registration was completed, I had to face getting behind the wheel to park the rig. Driving on a road, even a narrow, winding road, is a snap when compared to parking. My assigned space had an ocean view that required that I simply pull straight in. But the angle also required jockeying backwards and forward a couple of times before I would be properly positioned in the site. I had not yet used reverse. The idea was out of the question. I'd had enough new experiences for one day, and I simply refused to back up. I pulled into the space at such an extreme angle that I couldn't open any of the storage bay doors on the passenger side without hitting a post. The electrical, water, and sewer connections were accessible, and that was a good thing, because, come hell or high water, I wasn't moving the coach one inch. No how, no way. This is one thing my cat Butch and I had in common. We could both be very stubborn.

Once I was hooked up, I was able to sit down and absorb where I was. The view from my windshield was breathtaking. There was endless ocean, sea gulls, and a perfect sunset with every shade of red spread on the panoramic horizon like a photograph on my living room wall, except it was real. I had almost forgotten what this was all about. I had wanted to sleep for a week, but now I didn't mind waiting at least until dark.

I decided to take the traditional sunset promenade around the park to check out the other coaches and evaluate the local weather. It's a ritual that takes place anywhere there's more than two RVs. Everyone sits outside, walks, and chats with neighbors and scopes out the general layout of the park. This is the RVer's version of happy hour. I had discovered the rituals and social rules of RVing on the road with Don, and now at least I had a good idea of what the scene was.

As I slowly walked deep in thought, with my wineglass in hand, I barely noticed a big party going on at one of the motor homes. A friendly voice brought me back to the here and now. "Hey, it looks like you need someplace to sit and drink that wine." The voice belonged to a young, good-looking guy who was sitting at his picnic table with five or six other magnificent young men, all either very drunk or on the way. As tired as I was, I couldn't resist being drawn into the celebration. They were on vacation, and they were going to party. I answered, "I could use a little company, thanks for the invitation." They all started asking me questions at once. It was fun being the center of attention. As I began to unwind and the wine loosened my tongue, I had a spurt of energy and got into the spirit of things. Before long, more people joined us, some with pots of chili, salads, popcorn, chips and dip, chicken, and even pizzas.

By the time I returned to my coach, I didn't have a worry in the world. If this was any indication of what was in store for me, then bring it on. I felt like a rock star. Apparently, there aren't a whole lot of single women in RV land. There hadn't been very many women partners in CPA firms either, but I managed that for seventeen years. Being the only woman in a man's world has never bothered me. Quite the contrary, it makes me feel bold and fearless. Having said that, I still wasn't going to face moving the coach until it was time to leave in a month. The time in Malibu passed quickly. Cathy and Dick, next door neighbors from Oxnard, delivered my car to me since I hadn't yet mustered the courage to tow it. As usual, I fell into a comfortable routine.

Evenings were spent around campfires with the regulars. Morning was my time for exercise and e-mail so I would be free for shopping in the afternoon. Being so close to Santa Monica and Los Angeles, I was able to spend lots of time with my Los Angeles friends and see all the new movies at Santa Monica's Third Street Promenade. The time spent in Malibu contributed nothing to my being an RVer, but it did give me a chance to catch my breath, relax a little, and begin to create a single woman's persona.

My next stop was Newport Beach. I was much less concerned about getting to Newport than I was at the prospect of backing out of my space. I had never backed up, and although I had a back-up camera, the image on my dashboard monitor was only 4.5 inches by 3.5 inches, and when the sun was bright, it was just 4.5 by 3.5 inches of glare. The side view mirrors weren't any help either, because there were more blind spots than view, and even a small error in judgment could be disastrous.

The night before I pulled out for Newport, I had stomach cramps, a headache, and awful diarrhea. I prayed this wouldn't happen every time I got ready to drive someplace. In my CPA days, this always happened before a big audit. It never interfered with my performance. In fact, by morning, I was usually completely cleaned out and ready to go. I deeply hoped my RVing performance would likewise be undiminished. I buttoned down everything that could move and prepared the coach for a day on the road. I walked around the perimeter of the coach and checked and double-checked the angle of the road and the angle of the rig. I got in and moved backward about one foot and then got out and physically examined my progress. In this way I inched my way out of my site until I was free of all obstacles. I was only slightly less rattled than when I'd arrived a month ago, but at least there were no more mountains and only about ten miles to the Santa Monica on-ramp to the I-10. The freeways were a breeze, and I planned on staying in the right-hand lane. No matter how long it took, I was going to relax and take it easy.

I was surprised at how much smoother things were going. Cathy and Dick promised to deliver my car to Newport Beach the following day. So, without further adieux, I was on my way. I handled the endless construction on PCH with my breath held, but at least I was able to force myself to keep my eyes open when oncoming trucks exploded past me with what felt like gale force gusts of wind. It was smooth sailing until I reached the I-5 interchange where traffic came to a complete standstill. At first I felt smug, having all the conveniences I would need to hang out as long as it took for traffic to clear, but after a few minutes, I realized that I really needed to use the bathroom. I tried to figure out if we were going to be stopped for minutes or hours, but there was no way to tell. Finally, I had no choice but to turn off the engine, put on the parking brake, and run to the bathroom to get relief. I could have only been gone for three minutes at the most, but by the time I got back to the driver's seat, there was pandemonium all around me. Apparently, traffic had begun to move as soon as I left the wheel, and cars were struggling to pass me and horns were honking. If looks could kill, my story would end here. But I was much too relieved to care.

The balance of my journey to Newport Beach was uneventful. I had good directions, an empty bladder, and enough fuel to arrive without having to face the ordeal of the gas station. Although that would be at the back of my mind for my entire stay at Newport Beach, for the moment, I had the wind at my back. What I'd learned about RVing so far could be summed up in a few words; pee on the run, and avoid all situations that could result in using reverse. Armed with these insights, I arrived at my super deluxe waterfront site at the Newport Dunes Resort in Newport Beach, California.

Chapter 14
Newport Beach, California— Surviving Armageddon

THE NEWPORT DUNES RV Resort was something to talk about. I chose a resort with a security gate and twenty-four hour security patrols for a reason. Y2K was coming, and even though I told myself that the Armageddon hype was a bunch of malarkey, I also knew that anything was possible, so better to be safe than sorry. Check-in was similar to checking into a fine hotel. It was winter, so the high season rate of ninety-five dollars a night was reduced to forty-five dollars, and even that seemed pretty steep to me. But when I heard that the price for the New Year's Eve celebration was almost four hundred big ones, I was shocked. Yes, it included dinner, a private fireworks display, and a basket of goodies for a celebration in the motor home, but even so, for that much money, I wasn't going to spend the evening alone.

I called Dan in Los Angeles and suggested that we spend New Year's Eve together. If it really was the end of the world, we may as well end it together; and if not, well, we may as well spend it together, too. Since he couldn't find any flaws in my logic, we agreed that he'd drive down to start the celebration in the early afternoon on New Year's Eve, spend the night on my reasonably comfortable couch, and take off for home (if there still was one) after breakfast on the first.

The week before, I began my own preparations for Armageddon. I dug up an old bottle of champagne I'd been dragging around with me for at least a year or two waiting for some celebration worthy of its quality. This seemed as appropriate as any. I bought two bottles of the best Merlot I could find, lots of canned goods, delicious snacks, and then I sat down to figure out how long I would be able to last in the motor home assuming everyone went crazy for a while. I calculated that the motor home was the safest place to be. My fuel tank was only half full, which meant I had fifty-five gallons of diesel. My generator automatically shut down when the fuel level reached a quarter of a tank, so my potential generator use would be about thirty gallons, which translated to thirty hours. It took two hours a day to charge the batteries for a full twenty-four hours of use, which gave me at least a couple of weeks and quite realistically much more, since there were many ways to preserve power to make the batteries last much longer. My propane tank was full. My refrigerator, which I always kept stocked with frozen fish, chicken, and veggies, would run for months. My stovetop was the only other accessory that used propane for power, so I didn't see any possible shortfall there. My fresh water tank was topped off with a hundred and ten gallons, so I wasn't worried about drinking water either. Of course, the question on everyone's mind was whether we were talking about a temporary power failure or out and out panic in the streets. I decided that I'd be fine for a minimum of two weeks, and possibly three or four. If things got really bad, I'd be in the same boat as lots of other folks, and I wasn't going to worry about it.

I toyed with the idea of getting more fuel, but the television was filled with frantic people running around at the last minute looking for emergency supplies, and the gas stations were a circus. I made the decision to stay put and not move until the hullabaloo calmed down. Dan arrived around noon, and it was great to just kick back and watch the birds and the water and talk about old times. Our friendship went back to 1980 when his life partner, Greg, brought me home for dinner. Dan and I started drinking to twenty years of history together. It wasn't long before the old videos of shared parties with now-deceased friends found their way to the VCR.

"It seems like yesterday," Dan said as we watched our more youthful images move across the television screen from an old St. Patrick's Day party at my now-sold condo in Westwood. "I was looking a little chubby that year, wouldn't you say?" I asked while I rolled my eyes in disbelief. We giggled at my funny hairdo and drunkenly reassured each other of how hot we were now in comparison to our earlier versions.

Unspoken by both of us was the awareness that Greg was missing from our get-together. He was no longer in our lives, as AIDS had taken him in his prime. But watching him now on the screen was more an affirmation of his memory than a downer for the evening's celebration. Greg had been my mentor, confidant, soul mate, and colleague. He was Dan's beloved life partner. The three of us were inseparable for fourteen years, and now, almost seven years after his death, neither of us had fully recovered from the loss. This was the history that held us together and made our choice to weather a potential doomsday together the only reasonable one. If anything was going to happen, it was going to happen to us both.

Once we finished with the videos, we were drunk enough to start on the munchies. My version of snacks was my finger pointing in the vicinity of the kitchen with words of encouragement. "Help yourself, Dan." He rolled his eyes at my lack of grace and went to see what we had. He found that when we added his goodies with my goodies, we'd eat ourselves into a coma long before our 7:00 p.m. celebration dinner started. So instead of gorging on food, we settled for more wine and a walk around the bay. Motor homes were arriving in droves, as much for the celebration as to be off the streets when the bewitching hour struck at midnight. As the time for dinner got closer, the excitement began to mount. But we'd have to wait until 9:00 p.m. to know if New York would make it without a problem.

"Come on. Let's go get some four-hundred-dollar food." I was such a gracious host. I couldn't help but remind Dan what dinner was costing. I might have contained my enthusiasm. The dinner looked like every buffet convention dinner ever served ... in 1950. We had asked for chicken. We got a rubberized version complimented with over-cooked veggies, rolls that were white, doughy things, topped off with some sort of chemical, for dessert. The cheap wine was plentiful, and there were those who were drinking it as if they had discovered the best new winery in the country.

Dan and I decided almost simultaneously that our goodies back at the coach were much better than this slop, and at least there, we'd have the privacy to kick back and zone out. We put lawn chairs on the sand right in front of the coach and brought out huge plates of crackers, cheese, fruit, nuts, and other munchies. We'd had plenty of wine, but now it was time to break out the champagne. After eating way too much, we started to get cold, and by now we were both pretty drunk. So the rest of New Year's Eve was spent in front of the television watching time zone after time zone usher in the New Year without incident. At midnight, the private fireworks display began. We bundled up in coats and blankets and watched as a full hour of pyrotechnics exploded so close to us we were sure we could reach out and touch them. It made up for the rubber chicken and any other real or imagined shortcomings of the evening. When we both passed out in our respective beds, it was with a feeling of happy security. We would live another day to tell this tale. It was not Armageddon. We were not going to be eating canned goods for a month. This was just another New Year's Day. Welcome to the year 2000.

January was windy and rainy with very cool evenings, but I was comfortably warm with my furnace running almost constantly. I never gave fuel consumption a thought. I knew the generator couldn't run unless there was at least a quarter tank of fuel, so I assumed that the furnace, which also ran on diesel, had a similar cut off. I prepared for my next destination, Palm Springs, where I would spend a couple of months at the prestigious Outdoor Resorts in Indio. The rental fees were outrageous, but the stock market hadn't completely tanked, and I was ever the optimist that it would all bounce right back. On the morning that I was preparing to leave, I started the engine and was flabbergasted to see the fuel gauge needle start to move. Within seconds, it was below empty. I had occasionally checked the fuel gauge but didn't realize that it didn't operate without the ignition on. I had wondered why the needle was at quarter mark for so long but thought the furnace just used a very small amount of fuel.

This was impossible. I'd been indoctrinated from day one to never let the coach run out of fuel. The only way to restart the engine would be with an expensive service call to pump the air out of the fuel lines. And here I was with an empty tank. I tried the ignition and by some miracle, the engine fired right up. I was so preoccupied with the fuel shortage that I backed out of my site with no drama and carefully followed my directions to the nearest fuel station that carried diesel. I began my approach, but orange cones blocked the lane closest to the curb, making a lane change impossible. It was now or never. I turned the wheel, flattened a couple of orange cones, and pulled into the station. Thank goodness I was still traveling without a tow car. Cathy and Dick had promised one more car delivery to Palm Springs. In the future, I'd be on my own. But today, I was grateful beyond words that I didn't have a car to deal with. Once I was in the station, I yelled out the window to an attendant for directions to the diesel pump. He motioned me around to the other side, and when I made the turn, to my horror, my fuel tank was on the wrong side. I would have to turn around. There was no one to help me, and I could almost hear the fuel disappearing each moment I delayed. I used the foot by foot method. I pulled forward into the alley and then began to back up foot by foot as far down the alley as I could so that I would be able to make a fresh entrance into the service station from the correct direction. It took a good ten minutes to back up about fifty feet, but eventually, I was positioned properly and began pumping fuel.

I was astonished as the pump indicator passed ninety gallons and continued past one hundred gallons. The tank registered full with 106 gallons. I had no idea how much fuel I could carry, but I'd erroneously thought it was a 104 gallons. Later, when I checked the owner's manual, I found that I carried 112 gallons of diesel fuel. I had been down to six gallons. I was on my way to Palm Springs a wiser woman. From that day forward, I vowed to start searching for fuel when the tank hit the one-half mark. I could be so naïve.

Chapter 15

Palm Springs and Preparing for Some Real Traveling

On the drive to Palm Springs I discovered cruise control. It was the first opportunity I'd had to drive the speed limit without the constant stop and go of traffic. The whole driving thing was getting to be less and less traumatic. I still had heart-stopping anxiety when it came to backing up and getting fuel, but with any luck, it could only get better, right? As I pulled into the Indio Outdoor Resorts Park, I was impressed with the beauty of the grounds. There were gardens with flowers and lights everywhere. The *Trailer Life Directory* touted a fitness room and a place to get e-mail. Once I was registered, I found that I wasn't allowed to use the fitness room because I wasn't an owner, and the e-mail hookup could only be used in five-minute intervals and there were always people waiting to get online. And there was a two dollar a day electricity charge in addition to the $1,250 per month rental fee. But most daunting of all, all of the sites were back-in sites. I chastised myself for being so fearful. After all, people back into these sites every day. Why was I making such a big deal out of it? I found my site, and again, no one was around to help. I started backing into my space and missed the opening entirely. I pulled forward, and tried again. This time I almost took out a light pole. Finally, on the third try, I was in. Just as I was finishing up with the same painstaking technique of getting out and checking my progress and then proceeding another foot or two, a man passing by stopped and asked if I needed help. It was nice, but I'd already done it myself. I didn't need anyone. *So there*, I thought as I stood a little taller and felt quite satisfied with myself.

I'd been so focused on getting parked that I'd ignored the other coaches in the park. Now that I was in and settled, I took a walk and had a hard time keeping my mouth closed. The park was at least 90 percent Prevost Coach conversions. The starting price for these babies was three quarters of a million, with many valued well over a million. I was accustomed to the friendliness of my neighbors in the parks so far, and I approached each person I met with an open enthusiasm and admiration for their beautiful vehicles. Unfortunately, I had no idea I had landed on Planet "I have more than you, so get lost." The most blatant example of this happened almost immediately. I work out almost every day, and since I wasn't allowed to use the fitness room in the park, I set up my exercise equipment on my patio, popped a workout video into the VCR installed in my outside storage bay, and proceeded to do a Yoga workout. My next door neighbor, a dapper gentleman of about seventy, came over and was having an animated conversation with me for fifteen or twenty minutes until he asked me what kind of landscaping I was planning for my site. I laughed and said what turned out to be fateful words. "I'm just a tenant. But I'll be here for a couple of months." My neighbor turned on his heel, never said another word, and walked away. I frequently caught him watching me work out from his coach window, but he never spoke to me again. After all, I was just a tenant.

My lack of social life at the park wasn't an issue, since I had a million things to do in order to prepare for my first trip north to Bend, Oregon, for a new windshield. The Beaver factory was willing to replace my cracked one, but only if I drove to Bend to have it installed. There were so many things to get my mind around. First, I needed to have a tow bar installed and figure out how to tow a car. Then I had to decide on a route that would be snow free, flat, and without two-lane roads. After researching for days, I found there was no such animal. I was going to be driving up Highway 97 into Bend, and for me, this was scary stuff. But before I could even get on Highway 97, I had to drive through the entire state of California and over the infamous California Grapevine mountain pass. The evening news was frequently filled with images of trucks lined up for miles waiting for unexpected snowstorms to clear so that they could proceed over the pass. Since I would be traveling north in early March, snow would be a possibility when I arrived in this region. I pushed visions of driving in snow as far out of my mind as I could. I'd deal with it when I had to, but not one minute sooner.

By some quirk of luck, one of the RV technicians from Bend was working the winter season in Palm Springs doing freelance repairs for the dealership that sold me my motor coach. He was available to install my tow bar and to give me instructions on what to do with it once I had it. Life is filled with people who come and go in our lives, and Mike was one of those wonderful acquaintances who seemed to show up every now and then just when I needed him the most.

Mike came out and wired the brake lights on the car to work while it was being towed, and I got my lesson on the correct way to connect, disconnect, and tow a car. The entire process took less than an hour, and when he left, I realized that I had nothing else left to delay my departure. It was time to leave for Bend. The umbilical cord with Cathy and Dick was going to be broken. My friends in LA wouldn't be there to console me and cheer me on. Once I left the Palm Springs area, I was going to really be on my own. As I put the coach in drive and slowly stepped on the accelerator, a neighbor waved enthusiastically at me. At first I thought he was waving good-bye, but when three or four more men joined him, I stopped to find that I'd left the emergency brake on the tow car. I had only driven about a hundred feet, but I'd left an incredible skid mark.

Another neighbor came over to check the tow bar connection and to help me stop the bleeding on my hands from when I connected the tow bar initially. He showed me how to cross the safety cables to avoid flipping the car if it should accidentally disconnect and bandaged the place where I'd pinched a piece of flesh clear off my thumb. I did one last safety check, and I was ready for takeoff. It was nice to see that these folks did have a heart after all.

As I drove down the I-10, I found my exit for the first night's stop, or at least the next best thing. My directions said, "Exit on Highway 126 west," but there was no indication that there was such an exit, so I decided to exit at Highway 126 east and find a turnaround, so I'd then be heading west. Pretty slick, huh? I miraculously found a safe place to turn around and drove west, with the addresses getting closer and closer to my destination, until the road came to a dead end. When I tried to turn around again, this time in a business's small parking lot, I misjudged the turn and was stuck, unable to go forward or backward. I tried to disconnect the car, but the angle of the turn had the tow bar locked too tight. I pulled, pushed, hammered, and twisted every exposed connection, but it looked like I was going to be there for a long time unless I found help. It was time to call for roadside assistance, but where in the world was I? Inconveniently, it was 5:00 p.m., and I was blocking all of the employees' cars. I asked one of the men staring at the rig in disgust for the names of the cross streets so I could call for help, and he just put his hand out for the keys. I was jabbering about how backing up would bend the tow bar, and that my cats were inside, and not to let them out, and on and on. He just ignored me, but as he stepped inside the rig, he said, "I drove an eighteen wheeler for twenty years. Don't worry." True to his word, after about thirty minutes of inching back and forth with miniscule progress on each try, the coach was clear and ready to go. I was grateful beyond words. In my efforts to loosen the tow bar, I'd acquired a few more cuts and bruises, but they weren't bleeding now, so I was ready to find my elusive exit.

I telephoned the reservation office at the RV park and was surprised to find that the exit for Highway 126 west was about ten miles up the road from the exit for Highway 126 east. Who knew? With new directions, I finally arrived safe and sound in a lovely RV park with lots of promise. I had visions of dinner in a nice restaurant, and then back to the coach for a shower and a good night's sleep. Apparently, with all that rocking back and forth to free the coach in the parking lot, the tow bar was stuck regardless of the angle, and there was no freeing it. I'd need to try the hammer routine again and pound it free, but it was already dark, and digging out tools and working by flashlight didn't sound like a viable solution. I moved on to hooking up the electric, water, sewer, and cable television connections but only succeeded in finding the electric, water, and sewer outlets. Although the park brochure listed twenty cable television stations, the connector was not to be found. It was much too late, and I was much too tired to make a federal case out of it. I tried to find a satellite signal for the television, but the surrounding trees weren't cooperating. So with no television, no car, and no restaurant, I satisfied myself with a dinner of peanuts and wine, and then took a vitamin pill, hoping it would all balance out in my stomach.

The coach was almost out of fuel, as I had long ago abandoned the naïve delusion that I would be able to obtain fuel whenever the tank was half empty, but having said that, I still felt that the problem would be easy to remedy in the morning. And although I felt like I'd been beaten to a pulp, my car was just a useless appendage, and I was bored silly with no television, I realized that remarkably, I was having fun, in some weird, masochistic way. The next day was sunny and warm. I was up early, and other than having a slight hangover from drinking wine on an empty stomach, I was ready to tackle getting on the road. The first thing that had to be done was to lubricate the transmission on the tow car. This is much easier than it sounds. All that's required is to start the engine and move the gearshift to each position for one or two minutes. What could be simpler? When I walked back to the tow car, I found that I'd left the key in the "accessory on" position all night. The battery was dead. Since I can't tow the car without lubricating it, I thought I'd disconnect the car, take the coach to get fuel, and then come back and tackle getting the car battery charged.

When I went to open the storage bay door to find my tools, it was jammed stuck. The bay door had slid out of alignment, and I couldn't reach anything inside. I'm a pragmatic woman. Problems exist only to be solved, and I was going to take care of this one way or the other. I went inside, got an oven mitt and a meat cleaver, and started to pound away at the door to move it back into alignment. By now, I was a curiosity in the park. People were gathering around at a safe distance watching me pounding away at the side of the coach. Finally, a gentleman came over with a toolbox, and after I explained the entire series of events, he removed the door, realigned it, got the hammer, freed the tow car, and charged the car battery. All I can say is, but for the kindness of strangers.

By now it was noon and time to check out. I filled up at the Shell station and looked forward to an easy day of driving to Manteca, California, where I was meeting a driving instructor for a private lesson. While I was pumping fuel, I fell into a casual conversation with a bus driver at the next pump. "How far is it to the Grapevine?" I asked. I was hoping it was north of Manteca so that I wouldn't have to tackle mountain grades until after my driving lesson. He gave me a puzzled stare, and said, "You're there." At first, I felt my stomach spasm and my heart palpitate wildly, but then I thought, *Why not? I made it this far without lessons; I can get over a mountain.* And I did. I drove over the mountain pass, arrived unscathed at the next RV park, registered without a problem, and missed the power pole by at least two inches as I made a perfect landing in my appointed site. The satellite television worked. The tow bar worked. The Honda worked. I felt in control for the first time, enough so that I made a salad for dinner then curled up with a glass of wine and watched television. It felt just like I was at home.

Chapter 16
Fear of Reverse

I HAD HANDLED my worst nightmares with some degree of grace, and now it was time to deal with my fear of reverse. I registered for a private driving class, and when I spoke to the driving school owner, I repeatedly asked if backing up into a campsite would be part of the program, and I was assured that it would be. The class was scheduled at an abandoned airstrip in Rio Vista, California, just outside Manteca, and I was instructed to stay at the nearby Sandy Beach County Park where I would meet my instructor. What a jewel of a park. I had a very large pull-through site with a beautiful view of the lake. The whole process of getting from park to park was becoming just a regular day on the road. I was doubly excited to arrive, as I had a dinner date with a friend I'd met through a personal ad in *Highways Magazine*. This would be our second meeting, and although the first time had been okay, it had also been far from exciting. George was a quiet man with lots of personal baggage. He was a little guy, just barely taller than my five-foot-three. You can imagine my suspicions when he told me he was living with his first ex-wife because he needed help with their son who he had custody of and that he was still hung up on his second ex-wife, who wouldn't have anything to do with him.

But we were planning on caravanning, not marrying, so I was happily anticipating a nice dinner. It would be a great change of pace for me. It was an opportunity to put on my best dress, high heels, and makeup. I hadn't gotten all gussied up for such a long time that it felt a lot like Halloween. Dinner started out a bit strained, but once we got the first glass of wine down, things loosened up a bit, and it became apparent that we had the potential for at least a friendship. "I can't wait to get on the road," George explained. "I haven't had the motor home out in almost a year." He did have a nice smile, and it was fun to speculate about our upcoming trip. "I'd really like to go all the way to the east coast and down to Florida. I'm researching my family's genealogy, and I need to eventually make it to south Florida to check the town records in several places I may have had family."

My experiences and background were much different. "I can't go back any further than my grandparents. I'm truly interested in hearing about what you've found." And I meant it. We continued filling each other in on our pasts, our present, and our dreams of the future, but it was getting late, and I had to find my way back in the pitch black country night, and I was eager to get started. George walked me out to my car, and when I rolled down my window to say my final goodnight, he leaned in and gave me the gentlest, sweetest, most promising kiss I'd had in a long time. I hoped he wasn't as screwed up as his convoluted relationships implied. At 9:00 a.m. sharp, my instructor knocked on my door, ready to lead me to the airstrip. The lesson was pretty anticlimactic considering that I had already driven all the way from Palm Springs to Manteca. There wasn't going to be a lot he could tell me that I hadn't already figured out for myself. I kept asking him when we would practice backing up, and he kept promising me it would be soon, probably early the next day.

When it was time to leave the lesson, I asked Ron, the instructor, if he was going to meet me at the RV park in the morning. He blew me off and rattled off some vague directions and said, "Meet me here. It's just right up Main around the curve." I grabbed a pencil and asked him to draw me a map because I didn't have a very good grasp of where we were, especially since I'd followed him there and didn't pay a lot of attention to where we were going. "Oh, by the way, be sure to tow your car tomorrow. I want to adjust your mirrors properly, check out the tow bar installation, and watch you connect and disconnect the car." He drew me a map with arrows and Xs that resembled hieroglyphics, and before I could digest what he'd written, he was gone. For a brief moment, the map made some small measure of sense. As I set out the next morning, I was not very concerned about finding the airstrip. I was relaxed and looking forward to the lesson. I figured I'd recognize something along the way.

When I began looking for the entrance to the airstrip that corresponded to the X on my map, nothing looked familiar. I continued up a two-lane road, only to find myself in some really beautiful farm country, but nothing was even remotely familiar. I was able to pull over to the side of the road and go into my calm, analytical, "I can solve anything" mode. First, I got out my laptop computer and tried to pinpoint my location on my street atlas. But to find where you're going on a map, it's real helpful to have a clue as to where you are. Next, I tried my cell phone to call the instructor for help, and of course, there was no signal. My only real cause for concern was that I would have come all this way, put up with a full day of nonsense, and still I would miss my class on backing up. By now, I was convinced there were secrets known to only a few on how to get the back end of the motor home into a small RV campsite, and I wanted to know what they were.

It was time to find a turn-around. A few miles up the road, I spotted what looked like an abandoned farmhouse with a narrow dirt road around it. As I entered the road, I was thrilled when I was able to squeak by a tree here and a storage shed there until I was ready to turn left back onto the road I'd come up. The turn-around had positioned me with my front end at a ninety-degree angle to the road, but the tow car was at a sixty-degree angle to the coach and within inches of taking part of the barn with it. I wasn't concerned because I was planning an uneventful left turn and I was sure there wouldn't be any problem with the tow car. Traffic had begun to thicken, and cars were speeding from both directions, and my deserted little country road was turning into a major thoroughfare. It was getting close to 9:00 a.m. on a weekday, and obviously, this was a popular route for the locals to get to work. Finally, traffic cleared, and I confidently pulled out and began my left turn. Because the tow car was so precariously close to the barn, I needed to pull straight forward farther than planned until the car was clear. In doing so, I was blocking the lanes in both directions. I hadn't calculated how narrow those two lanes were, and when I saw the car clear the barn in my side-view mirror, I began to turn the wheel all the way to the left, and as I pulled forward, I ran out of road. There I sat, unable to go forward and unable to go backward. The front end of the coach was up against a tree on the other side of the road.

I got out of the coach to examine angles, clearances, and really just to give myself a chance to think. I'd been having so much trouble with the release on the tow bar that I didn't have to even try to disconnect the car at its current angle to know there was no way in hell. Through trial and error, I'd found that the only way the tow bar released was if the car was exactly behind the coach on a level surface. When I looked at the situation, I observed that the car was still at a sixty-degree angle, and the coach's rear end was up in the air, as the front end descended the driveway back onto the road. With a tree impeding my forward progress, I had no room to maneuver the front end of the motor home. Really, there was no solution, and nobody could get past me, but more and more people were accumulating every minute, and they weren't happy. By now I had my gloves on, and I was giving the appearance of disconnecting the car. No one approached me, and no one tried to help me. They were all dressed up in their going to work clothes, and hostility was thick in the air. The language was getting raw, and my frustration and embarrassment were physically painful. There was nothing to do but to back up. If the tow bar bent, then so be it. I couldn't sit here blocking traffic indefinitely. I started to back up, but the car got closer and closer to the barn and even worse, it was jack-knifing right into the left rear corner of the coach. I got out again and saw that I'd actually dented the car and the coach. My blood pressure was now off the charts. I could feel the blood all rushing to my brain, and I would have almost welcomed an aneurysm. At least then someone else would have to worry about moving the coach. At last, I had an epiphany. I could turn right and at least I'd be no worse off than when I'd started. It would just mean finding another turn around further up. Thank God I had backed up just enough to allow me to pull to the right and get back on the road. By now, I was pretty shaken up and fully prepared to drive in this direction until I got to the next state.

About a mile up the road, I came to a really huge turn-around marked for school buses. The size was ample for an eighteen-wheeler. Now, here's a lesson for life if I've ever seen one. I gave up too soon. What I was looking for was just one little mile further along my path, but I chose to improvise instead of holding the course. This would prove to be just about the most important lesson in RVing so far. Don't guess. Wait until you're sure. And don't give up. Eventually, there will be a safe place to do whatever it is that needs to be done. As I began to retrace my steps in order to find the elusive entrance to the airstrip, the instructor was driving up the road toward me. It had finally dawned on him that I was probably in trouble and needed assistance. He led the way back to the airfield, and we commenced with the final day of class. I might as well have stayed in bed. He had me drive backward using a white line on the road as my guide. *So much for the secrets of reverse,* I fumed to myself.

Chapter 17
Mount Shasta to Medford—
Falling into a Routine

I LEFT RIO VISTA and headed to the Elks Lodge in Carmichael, California, where I would meet George and the other couple we would be caravanning with once we got to Canada. Although meeting Larry was okay, his wife Linda gave me a cold chill that reached deep into the marrow of my bones. Something was very off center, and I wasn't looking forward to traveling with her. When I mentioned to George that I felt uncomfortable around her, he said, "I try to stay as far away from her as possible, but she's my best friend's wife, what can I do?"

We agreed to meet at an RV park just outside of Medford, Oregon, the first week of June, after I completed my maintenance in Bend, Oregon, and after he wrapped up some business projects. We seemed reasonably compatible, and I was still excited to have someone to share this awesome experience with. I had plans to stop in Mount Shasta on the way north to meet another potential caravan partner. He was retired, my age, and full timing in an old Beaver Marquis. He sounded nice on the phone, and I was excited to see if he was more interesting than George. I used a single's Web site online called Match.com, and so far I had met a long line of nice but inappropriate men. But as with everything else in life, it only takes one success to make me a winner, and I was having fun meeting lots of interesting single men along the way. I wasn't very concerned about my safety, as I met most prospective male companions in RV parks where it was safe, and people surrounded us. Worst case scenario would simply be to start up the engine and take off for a different location.

The town of Mount Shasta was charming, and the surrounding area was full of hiking trails, rivers, and wildlife. My new friend and I spent a couple of days getting to know each other as we hiked and shared meals, and by the time I was ready to hit the road, George was looking better and better. Maybe it's just par for the course, but all the men I'd met so far RVing were so tight they squeaked when they walked, and my new friend was leader of the pack in that regard. It was now time to start up Highway 97, all two lanes of it, up to the high desert where Bend was located at an elevation of about 4,000 feet. I didn't know what to expect, but I'd grilled every person I met on the road about the level of difficulty. I even considered driving all the way up I-5 to Portland and then south down Highway 97 into the town of Bend, but any way you looked at it, I needed to get to 4,000 feet on a two-lane road.

The weather was getting overcast, and since this was still only April, there was always a chance of snow, but rain was more likely. My appointment at the factory had been made several months earlier, and being on time was an absolute requirement. I planned on taking two days to get from Mount Shasta to Bend, and in hindsight, that's pretty funny, since it's only 220 miles, but at the time, it was all I could handle. The first RV park on Highway 97 was charming, with large sites and a huge circular drive. When I registered, the woman at the desk said, "Just turn around in the drive and take the first road to your space." I looked out the window and asked, "Isn't there another way? I'll never make that turn. Maybe I should disconnect the car now while I'm relatively straight."

"No, no, don't be silly. Rigs make that turn all the time. Just go ahead and pull right around." You'd think I would have learned by now. But in my defense, this would be the last time I would ever let anyone tell me that I could do something with the coach that my better judgment told me I couldn't. But this was still early in the game, and I still didn't feel that I knew as much as anyone else. To make a long story short, I tried, failed, disconnected with great difficulty because of the now difficult angle, and got settled on a riverfront site. The park itself was without any ambiance at all, but if I put my lawn chair next to the river, I could imagine that I was out in the wilderness as long as I didn't turn around.

Just before sunset, I did my usual promenade around the park to check out the rigs and the people, and as usual, I was invited for cocktails, and the evening passed pleasantly. When I woke, it was raining just hard enough to make getting ready to pull out a big mess, but not hard enough to make driving dangerous, or so I hoped. I did call the RV park in Bend to ask if I could cancel my reservation if it continued raining, and after about thirty seconds of silence, I was politely told that rain didn't qualify as a refundable emergency. So much for that idea. I'd just have to bite the bullet and hit the road. Once on the road, the rain became a blinding torrent. It was like being in a car wash. The windshield wipers couldn't go fast enough, and there was no place to pull over, so I just continued driving through the mountain passes at a snail's pace. I could see the brake lights of a vehicle in front of me, and I used that as my guide the entire way. After an hour of this, the downpour diminished to a nice, hard rainfall. I began to get the feel of the road and found that my 36,000 pounds of equipment weren't going to float away. I was able to stay at about forty miles an hour, and by the time I reached Crown Villa RV Resort in Bend, I was relaxed and ready to wait for my factory appointment in three days.

I felt like I was getting a good handle on this maintenance thing. I had cracked my windshield when I leveled the coach, and the factory had agreed to replace it at no charge since it was a design flaw and not something I had done. The windshield replacement was a painless procedure, and before I knew it, I was on my way to Medford, Oregon, to wait for George to join me. Medford is a busy town just twelve miles from the center of the Oregon Shakespeare Festival in Ashland. I chose an RV park in Phoenix right smack dab between Medford and Ashland. This gave me easy access to the shopping malls and city amenities in Medford and the culture and small town charm in Ashland. I would be staying about a month, since George wouldn't be ready to leave Carmichael until after he took care of his own personal business, and that was fine with me. I was looking forward to exploring the area. It was surrounded by endless tourist attractions, and I was chomping on the steering wheel to be a tourist. Once George arrived, my other friends from LA would also be joining us for a week of theatrical performances at the festival.

Arriving in nearby Ashland is like stepping back to the sixties and seventies. The town is filled with a variety of art galleries, shops selling Native American artifacts, hippie garb, health-conscious restaurants, and students traveling from everywhere. The three theaters that make up the festival are central to the town's existence. People come from around the country to enjoy these world-class performances not only showcasing Shakespeare's finest uniquely staged and directed, but also classic theater productions and original works. The three theaters include a small, intimate venue, an outdoor Elizabethan theater, and a larger indoor theater. I had been meeting Dan and several of our other friends for the last several years, and each year had been better than the last, but this was my first visit in the motor coach. George was in for a real treat, as this would be his first taste of Ashland.

Jacksonville is just up the road from Ashland, and I did the tourist routine on Mother's Day. While I was walking up and down the streets checking out the museums and old shops, I found the town cemetery. Thinking it would be appropriate to walk among the graves and say a prayer for my mom, I hiked up the hill to take a look around. There was an arrow that said "Jewish," and I had to see what that was all about. I was treated to row after row of Jewish gravestones from the 1800s. Who would have imagined that there was such a thing as a Jewish cemetery in this tiny historic town from the gold rush era? There was a large monument dedicated to all who lay there, and many people had come before me, and as tradition dictates, placed a pebble in memory of their loved ones on the surface.

I found my own piece of stone, carefully placed it on the monument, and said a prayer. I sat quietly and meditated for a few minutes, remembering the good and the bad. I had always wished that she hadn't died when I was so young, but many of Mom's lessons stayed with me. She always pushed me to go conquer the world. She wanted me to go where no one in our family had ever dared before. She wanted me to have and do everything she didn't, and I was definitely doing my best to make her vision mine. I had long ago forgiven her for making me move out so many years ago, and I was left only with a daughter's regret at not having a mother to share all of life's confusion with.

In the middle of this fascinating backdrop sat Phoenix, Oregon. It was a town so small that it was best known for the outlet mall right next door to the Holiday RV Park. I couldn't have chosen a better place to stay. Larry and Joyce, the owners, adopted me and found solutions to any problem I could create. If something broke, they were on the phone to the appropriate repair person in minutes and the problem was solved. The park has a small creek that runs through it. My site was right on the water, and there was a fantastic gym just a couple of miles up the road. As excited as I was to get started on the adventure with George, I also was finding that spending an extended piece of time in one place enhanced life on the road.

Chapter 18
Caravanning—the Good, the Bad, and the Ugly

GEORGE AND I had debated whether we should both tow our cars since we'd probably be doing most activities together. But two adults in their fifties don't give up something as central to their independence as their automobiles that easily. So, in the end, George towed his car, too. We spent the week of the Shakespeare festival meeting my friends before the performances for lunch or dinner, and the mornings were spent reading the paper, lounging under the awning with a book, and enjoying each other's company. Just a couple of days before we were planning to pull out, I had an accident with my Honda. I was driving home from a doctor's appointment when an ambulance turned left in front of me at an intersection. I had the green light, and luckily I had my seat belt on. There were no emergency lights and no warning. All of a sudden, a very large white vehicle was in my path. I tried to think of every driving lesson and tip I'd ever had, as I calmly checked for an escape path. Not finding one, I decided the best thing I could do was to keep the car as straight as possible to avoid hitting any pedestrians or nearby cars, and I pushed down on the brake with all my strength. The impact was at a ninety-degree angle right into the rear wheel of the ambulance. My airbag didn't inflate, but my seat belt held fast. When the dust settled, I was unhurt but badly shaken. I got out of the car, and two witnesses came running over to me.

"We saw it all. He turned right in front of you. Are you okay?" Both witnesses were unrelated, but they took care of me as a team. The woman held my hand, and the man wrote both of their names and phone numbers down for me

I wasn't injured, but the car had $6,200 worth of damage, and it was going to be weeks and weeks before it would be fixed. Now what was I supposed to do? I mentioned my dilemma to Joyce and Larry at the RV park, and they immediately said, "Don't worry about the car. Go on your trip, and when the car's done, we'll go get it and just leave it parked here until you come back this way." Their generosity solved my problem. The question of how many tow cars were too many was also solved. George would be the designated driver, and I would have the luxury of doing our trip together without a tow car. Talk about finding the silver lining.

It was time to hit the road with George in his motor home and me in mine. We agreed that I would follow behind since I was the slower of the two. George's rig was only thirty-four feet and about half my weight. He had a gas engine with a much smaller fuel capacity than mine, so he would be setting the pace and stopping for fuel as needed. George and I settled into a comfortable routine wherever we stayed. Without much discussion, an intimacy developed that was lacking in romantic sparks but satisfying and comfortable for both of us. We took turns getting the coffee and paper in the morning. We'd split up for our morning workout routine and then plan whatever tourist traps we wanted to visit in the early afternoon. Breakfast was whatever we each threw together, but lunch and dinner soon fell into my realm. It didn't take long before I noticed that not only was I doing all the cooking, but I was also doing all the buying of groceries. Occasionally, he'd take me out to dinner, but even then it was frequently Dutch. But in spite of his shortcomings, he was easy to be around and very laid-back company. I rationalized his selfish behavior by convincing myself that it was fun having a travel companion. Sharing a couple of meals a day seemed an inconsequential price for that luxury.

Our first scheduled extended stay was Newport, Oregon. The drive was my first chance to try my skills on a real back road. Highway 20 to Highway 138, which then went straight to the ocean, was heart stopping. It rained on and off as we drove through a road canopied with trees more lush than I'd seen east of Hawaii. It reminded me of the New Zealand rain forest. Rainbows were visible at every break in the foliage, and as we drove along the curving, hilly road to the ocean, we had relaxed chatter between us on our CBs. We both kept repeating, "Wow, did you see that?" or "Quick, look over there on the right, that bird is amazing." Once we arrived at the Pacific Outdoor RV Resort, George showed great restraint when he learned the price of the sites. Even he was swept away with the beauty and possibilities of this trip together. A footpath led right down to the rocky beach. We hiked the beach, explored the lighthouses along the coast, and even took the lighthouse tours. Climbing up the narrow stairwells and peering out into the ocean, we shared a nice, lighthearted camaraderie. No matter what we did or where we went, though, George had a wall around him that made everything somewhat strained.

The weather was cold and windy most of the time. Coastal June weather is commonly referred to as June gloom. At last we had a stretch of good weather, and I sprung for a coach wash by a local teenager. Forty dollars for a wash was really reasonable, and the coach was filthy. He told me he'd be back later that day since he had two or three coaches scheduled before me. Of course, just as I stepped into the shower, I looked up through the skylight and there he was. Oh hell, I thought. If he's never seen it before, he'll have the thrill of his life, and if he has, well there's nothing new here. I continued with my shower and heard him scurry away on the roof. When I was dry and dressed, I ventured out to see how he was progressing. He was bent over my left front tire with a big frown. "Lady, come take a look at this," he said. I bent down and found what looked like a zipper along the side of my tire. "This is going to blow any minute. I wouldn't drive even ten feet on this," he warned. I was so grateful, I gave him a generous tip and started a marathon of phone calls that would eventually get Goodyear to replace and install my new tire. Since we were planning a long trip into Canada, I was relieved to get the tire fixed now when there wasn't any time pressure or another couple waiting around for me.

Finally, we were ready to go north across the Canadian border to Peace Arch and meet Larry and Linda. I began dreading the approaching intrusion, because I knew the dynamic between George and I was going to change dramatically. But all thoughts of Larry and Linda were soon to vanish as the border crossing turned from casual to intense. As I approached the booths, I didn't notice any difference in width between any of the lanes. I just fell in behind George's rig. I hadn't considered that he had a narrow-body RV, which was ninety-six inches wide, while I had a wide-bodied model at a hundred and two not counting mirrors. George pulled through easily after what seemed like ten seconds of questioning. When it was my turn, I pulled forward and heard a high-pitched scraping sound of metal on metal. It sounded like the entire side of my coach was damaged. I stopped dead in my tracks, hoping the border patrol would help me, and sure enough, a couple of uniformed officers shoved my mirrors all the way in to the coach and started directing me through. I just barely squeaked by, and now the real fun began.

"Who is the owner of the vehicle?" the first officer asked gruffly.

"I am," I answered respectfully.

"Who else is inside?" another guard asked with a cold blank stare.

"It's just me."

Now a third guard came over to continue the interview. "Who else is inside?"

"No one's inside. It's just me." Again, I smiled sweetly.

"Do you have any weapons?"

Hell, I wouldn't even carry mace for protection out of fear I'd end up spraying myself. "No sir, I don't have any weapons of any kind."

I was getting nervous. George was long gone, and I was feeling very vulnerable. I didn't fit the proper profile. Subsequent to my crossing, I discovered that there were very real terrorists apprehended right here at the crossing between Blaine, Washington, and Canada. The knowledge that this border was closely and suspiciously watched might have motivated me to cross elsewhere, not because I was guilty of anything, but just because I know I am unusual and create curiosity where ever I go. Regardless of my innocence, I appeared to the border patrol as potentially dangerous.

"Why are you going to Canada?"

I froze. I couldn't remember for the life of me why I wanted to go there. I stuttered something about friends.

"What are their names and addresses? How long are you staying?"

These were all reasonable questions. And I couldn't answer a single one. I just sat there looking like he'd asked me for the secret formula for sending a rocket to the moon. I finally spit out, "I don't know."

And now guard number four approached. "Whose rig is this?" he asked suspiciously.

"Mine."

"Who else is inside?" he asked.

"No one is inside except me." I finally found my voice and tried to explain that I was caravanning with my friend, and we were meeting another couple at the RV park in Peace Arch, but he wasn't buying any of it. The guards walked away and huddled. By now all I wanted was to get out of there, but I couldn't back up through that narrow lane, and I was sure they'd shoot me anyway if I tried.

A female guard came over and started again, this time with a smirk on her face. "Whose rig is this?"

By now I was seriously upset. I tend to get blotchy red spots all over my face and neck whenever I'm excited or sad or happy or agitated in any way. I was bright red by now, which only made me more nervous, as I feared this would scream guilt to all who saw me. I kept waving the registration and insurance papers at each of the guards who questioned me, but no one wanted to see them. They were so convinced that I couldn't possibly own, operate, and care for this rig on my own that I was tried and convicted as I sat there. And I sat there a long time as they conferred, huddled, and debated what to do with me, and then as suddenly as they'd begun, the interrogation was over. Without a single word, the female of the group waved me through. But my mirrors were still pushed tight against the coach, and my lane exited directly onto the fast left lane of the highway. I had zero visibility. I got out of the coach, and with all my hundred and eight pounds, I pulled against the mirrors and was unable to make them move even an inch. The patrol guards had turned their backs on me and were now pouncing on a new piece of meat. I decided to try and call George on the cell phone, but it just rang and rang until the recorded message asked me to leave a message. I blurted out something that made little sense. I had directions to the park, but driving the coach without mirrors was impossible, yet I couldn't think of anything else to do.

As I pulled out into traffic, I found myself in the extreme left lane of a highway with four lanes in each direction. Somehow, I needed to cross four lanes in sixty-mph traffic with zero visibility. I put on my turn signal and started changing lanes at a heart stopping ten mph. My theory was that going as slowly as I was, anyone would be able to get around me. Eventually, I made it over to the extreme right lane, and I hoped that there would be someplace to pull over and have a little nervous breakdown before I continued. No luck— there was nothing but narrow dirt shoulder. My cell phone rang, and I answered it on the first ring. Thank God it was George. I started rambling hysterically, but he abruptly interrupted me.

"Smoky is having seizures. I've got my hands full. I'm on the side of the road. I'll wait for you." Click. Perfect, we were both bordering on hysteria. His obnoxious, overbearing, ill-trained dog now had medical problems. Oh goody. I pulled up behind him a few miles up the road, and he was unable to free my mirrors without tools. I would have to drive all the way to the park down very narrow two-lane roads without mirrors. This was an accident waiting to happen. It was almost impossible to judge where my front left corner was on the road without mirrors. Every time a car came past me from the opposite direction, I cringed just waiting for the sound of metal on metal. I still hadn't had a chance to check the damage on the side of the coach from the border crossing fiasco, and by now my imagination had gone wild.

We arrived at the RV park, and it was wonderful. What a relief! The site was twelve dollars a night, including a private phone line. The park was tree-lined, and the sites were spacious. Once I got into my space, we were able to get the mirrors adjusted and assess the damage to the side of the coach. Miraculously, the scraping sound had been my automatic step scraping against the concrete wall. There was absolutely no damage. After quite a bit of wine, the memory of the border crossing began to recede. Canada was going to be awesome and cheap. The people in the registration office were gracious. The people in the neighboring coaches were gracious, and Linda and Larry weren't scheduled to arrive for a week. George and I had some more time for just the two of us, and it was a week filled with sightseeing, relaxed dinners at home, and lots of fun snuggling. George started to loosen up a bit, and I think we were both having a great time.

It was an ill wind that blew Larry and Linda into town. At first Larry struck me as an okay kind of guy, but, after all, he was married to witch Linda. Whatever I did to offend this woman was never addressed directly. She chose instead to act civilly when anyone else was around and ignore me completely at all other times. I could see why the three of them were such close friends. They took cheap to a whole new level. For the three of them, it was a competition. Once we left the comforts of Peace Arch, I learned that their favorite place to camp was in back alleys behind restaurants or behind gas stations or wherever they could get away with parking for free. One morning was particularly cold, and I put the generator on so I could run my furnace and take a shower. The cold got me up at 5:00 a.m., and Linda pissed and moaned all day long about how early I made her get up with my noisy generator.

Caravanning was horrible. George turned his entire attention to Larry and Linda and pretty much excluded me from everything. While we traveled, he no longer chatted with me on the CB but rather talked to Larry. If I had the audacity to make a comment over the CB, they just ignored it. Larry led the pack, and his driving was so erratic that it was very difficult to keep up. As we tunneled through the Canadian Rockies, he maintained a speed of at least seventy mph. When we reached flatter plateaus, he dragged along at fifty. When I jokingly asked him, "Hey, Larry, what's the deal? Why so slow on the flats and so fast on the hills?" he just gave me a dirty look and ignored me. I realize now that a good way to get up and down steep grades is to get a running start and use the momentum on the way down the grade to help get up the next one. But Larry wasn't in any mood to help me with an explanation. Both Linda and Larry only spoke to me if George was present. And then when they did speak, they were so insincerely sweet that I wanted to puke. The contrast of how accepting and embracing my friends were at the Shakespeare Festival and how truly hateful his were here on the road reconfirmed something I already knew. You really can judge a person by the company he keeps.

Chapter 19
To Banff, Bedlam, and Beyond

THE ROADS THROUGH the Canadian Rockies are engineered with tunnels snaking through the granite masses rather than the zigzagging switchbacks Americans are accustomed to. As I entered the first tunnel, a one-dimensional wall of black nothingness engulfed me as though I'd closed my eyes. The light beams from my headlights were swallowed entirely. As everything went black, I took my foot off of the accelerator and held my breath. I was afraid to go too slowly because there was traffic behind me, and they were probably just as blinded by the change in light as I was. As I clenched my body waiting for an impact from one direction or the other, the proverbial light at the end of the tunnel came into view. No other tunnel on Highway 1 had this strange blackout effect, thank goodness. But experiencing it even once may have permanently damaged my entire nervous system.

Because the roads don't zigzag around the mountains, but rather tunnel through them, the road has a constant up and down, rolling effect that creates a dance with the truckers. I learned early in my indoctrination that the truckers always have the right of way. They're under stress trying to meet tough delivery deadlines, and they don't need the added distraction of dealing with inconsiderate vacationers in huge motor homes rubbernecking at every spectacular view while driving forty mph in the passing lane. Generally, I was able to go faster up the inclines than the trucks due to my lighter weight, and the truckers were able to go faster as they descended due to their higher degree of confidence and added momentum from their extra weight. The ride took on a hypnotic rhythm as we jockeyed along, first, with me swinging past the trucks as we ascended, and then having them swing past me on the downgrade. On several occasions, I was separated from the other two coaches since they were much smaller and lighter than I was, and I had to hustle to catch up on the descent. Each time I tried to pass in the passing lane, the trucks would also be trying to get past the slower, larger vehicles. Several times I tried but just couldn't get my speed up because the truck in front of me was holding me back. A struggling truck in front of me noticed that he was holding me back. At the next opportunity, he stayed behind the slower vehicle and signaled me to pass them both. It may sound like a small thing, but for me, it was significant. A busy, stressed-out stranger understandably frustrated at his own difficulty in getting past our mutual obstacle moved aside and let me by.

Things between George and I got worse once we arrived at Banff National Park. George had become cohorts with Larry and Linda, and whatever fragile intimacy we had been developing was quickly dissolving. Now, whatever I did was cause for furtive glances between them and the rolling of eyes at my every comment. I'll never know exactly what happened, but the dynamic of George and I alone was delightful. It just couldn't coexist with his friends. George and I agreed to separate, but I was in the unhappy situation of being in Banff without a car. We decided to take his car up into Jasper to visit the ice fields and see all the sights on the way, partly as a way to take the edge off of the impending separation, and partly because we both wanted to see the Jasper ice fields. We still felt some remnant of our previous mutual affection, but rather than discuss what was happening between us, we turned our attention to our surroundings. The drive was too awesome to let a little thing like a break-up ruin our last day together.

Every turn in the road was more panoramic than the last. These were real mountains. They made the American Rockies look like large foothills, and photographs just couldn't do justice to what we were seeing. We stopped at every turn-off and every footpath on the way to Jasper. We didn't know what to expect, but when we arrived, we were a little bewildered. The huge ice field sat just a few feet across the street from the Tourist Information Center. Walking to the glacier was forbidden. Apparently, walking to the ice caused damage, but driving huge buses with oversized wheels on it was benign. Getting out of the bus and walking on the glacier was also benign. Go figure.

We each paid our twenty dollars for the tour, boarded the bus, and drove a hundred yards to the glacier. We were then allowed to get out, take pictures, and walk wherever we wished. Although the whole thing smacked of a tourist trap, this was a once-in-a-lifetime experience, and I thought, *Let the Canadians make a few bucks. This is something worth seeing.* As George and I drove back to Banff, neither one of us was willing to break the awkward silence. I suppose we were both tired from the long day on the road, but emotionally, we were also both ready to move on. Maybe Linda and Larry were just his excuse to end things without having to say anything about what he was feeling. Early on, he had confessed that he would do almost anything to avoid confrontation, and, once again, I had the opportunity to live and learn another one of life's lessons. Believe what people tell you when they describe themselves. If they say they're selfish or mean or inconsiderate, they probably know what they're talking about. And as my friend, Dan, pointed out to me in a quick phone call that morning, "George told you the truth about himself and you chose to ignore it. So don't act surprised now!"

The next morning, I got up, and without ceremony or good-byes I drove away from Banff National Park, George, and his buddies. I was surprised that what I felt was relief rather than sadness. We hadn't been together long, but after almost three months of daily life together, he'd become a pleasant habit, if not the love of my life. And now, the sense of freedom at not having to plan meals and consider someone else's needs began to tingle through me. And I liked it. Being alone was okay, but being without a car was going to be a problem. I'd just have to deal with that later. For now, it was time to move on.

Without anyone to follow, and having made no plans, I had to rely on the signs on the road to lead me to I-15 and, ultimately, Montana. Canadian signs are only useful if you already know where you are and where you're going. On leaving Banff, the first large town was Calgary. The highway goes right through the city, and watching for signs in morning rush hour traffic with three or four lanes in each direction is precarious at best. As I drove along in the right lane, a small sign on the side of the road marked the street I was looking for with a left arrow. There was no other warning, just turn left now. Luckily, I was able to get over in time, but knowing that wouldn't always be the case kept me nervous and clutching the wheel while I endlessly scanned the roadside for more hidden clues. Finally, the freeway entrance came into view, but instead of denoting north and south, it named two obscure towns that only Canadians would recognize with arrows in opposite directions. No visitor could possibly know which way to turn to get to Montana. But life was much easier without a tow car. I could take chances and make mistakes. Turning around was still a challenge but not one that caused distress. And luck seemed to be on my side, because when I guessed which way to turn, I found Montana.

When I approached the border at Sweet Grass, Montana, traveling south on I-15, I was prepared for the same horror I'd experienced coming into Canada, but there was nothing to fear here. Sweet Grass is an outpost surrounded by nothing. There were only two lanes at the border—one for trucks and one for cars. I had no hesitation in choosing the truck lane. As I pulled up, a border officer waddled over. He was easily four hundred pounds. He motioned for me to exit the coach, and without a word, pulled his hulk up my automatic step by hanging all his weight off of the coach door for leverage. I'd had the door repaired twice already when it got out of alignment, and my stomach clenched as I saw his massive body hanging from my delicately balanced door. It only took a second for me to come to my senses and join him inside my home.

"I've never seen the inside of one of these," he mentioned while he made himself at home examining the cabinetry and the other amenities throughout. His glance caught one of my sleeping cats and he began a whole cooing and gurgling conversation with Butch. "What a pretty boy. What kind of cat is it? He looks like a little cougar." He then moved to continue his examination of the contents of my cupboards while he waited for my answer.

"He's an Abyssinian. What are you looking for?" *What did he think I was smuggling in from Canada, a hockey player?*

"I've never seen one of these million dollar rigs," he elaborated on his first introductory comment by adding a monetary value. He must have realized that he was way out of line with that comment, and as he began to blush, he moved toward the door. I didn't bother correcting his bizarre assumption about the value of my rig, but I did take it as a clue to what might lay ahead with the locals.

I had crossed the border and found myself in the middle of desolate country. Now back on American soil, I decided to treat myself to breakfast at the first diner I found. Within minutes, I saw a perfect café with a dirt parking lot with room for at least five or six eighteen-wheelers. I pulled right in and realized that I could back up blindfolded and still not have any problem getting out. I turned on my generator and air conditioner so the kitties would be comfortable, and I strolled into the diner. Everyone turned and stared as I passed through the restaurant door. The waitress at the register nodded a greeting and spoke sparingly, "Sit anywhere." She vaguely gave a sweeping motion with the menu in her hand, indicating the entire restaurant, which was made up of six counter stools and four tables. I chose the only empty table and was happy to see that I was able to keep an eye on the motor home. I always felt better if I could keep it in my sight, especially someplace as isolated as this. The waitress took her time walking the few feet from the register to the table, and as she handed me the menu, she asked, "Whadayawant?"

"I'll need just a minute to decide." As I scanned the menu, I could see this wasn't going to be easy. The menu was missing everything that I eat. There was no nonfat milk for the oatmeal and no turkey sausage. I didn't see any egg substitutes, and I didn't want to eat any yolks.

Well Toto, we're not in Kansas anymore, I thought. I decided to order four eggs over hard and not eat the yokes, oatmeal without milk, only eat half, and herb tea. While I waited for the waitress to stop ignoring me because I'd caused her to wait for my order, I picked up a previously-read local newspaper off the counter and amused myself with news of the local rodeo. "Decided?" Ms. Talkative was back.

"I'd like four eggs over hard, no potatoes, and no toast. A few slices of tomato would be nice instead."

"No substitutions."

Great, now maybe Jack Nicholson was going to show up and order a chicken salad sandwich, hold the chicken, so that he could get an order of toast after the breakfast menu was pulled. "Okay, no problem. Also, I'd like oatmeal, no milk, no sugar, no raisins, just plain."

"We don't serve oatmeal after eleven o'clock." Her hand was on her hip, and the impatience was just oozing out of her.

"Then I guess I'll have wheat toast, dry, no butter, and no jelly, okay?"

"It's your stomach," she flipped back at me.

"Oh, and may I have some herb tea?"

"Lady, we just got coffee and regular tea. Which do you want?" The men at the other tables were now snickering.

"I'd like decaf coffee."

I buried my head in the newspaper and wondered what made me think this was going to be a pleasant experience. When my food came, it was everything I didn't want. The four eggs were over easy, so I couldn't separate the yolks from the whites. The eggs came with a large serving of hash brown potatoes swimming in grease. The four pieces of white toast where soaked in butter. And, the coffee was too old and burned for me to even guess if it was decaf or regular. I put ten dollars on the table and walked out. Once back in the coach, I held on to Butch and put my face deep into his fur as I breathed in his distinctive scent. There was something about his smell that always calmed me, and brought everything back into perspective. "Well, Butch, how about if I make myself exactly what I want." Butch purred loudly in a supportive response, as Sundance pushed his muzzle under my elbow to be sure he was included in the family hug, and I proceeded to make and enjoy my meal right there in the parking lot. I relished the idea that someone might have the audacity to tell me to move, and I was prepared with an impassioned speech about my civil rights, even though I was on private property and probably didn't really have any. But no one came. *Welcome home*, I thought. *Welcome back to the good old U. S. of A.*

Chapter 20

Sometimes It Really Feels Better to Be Alone

I REGISTERED FOR a week's stay at a lovely park just a few miles from the west entrance of Glacier National Park. Since my coach was too large to navigate the park's steep, narrow roads, I rented a car. I couldn't wait to take a long, quiet, solo hike. I've found that even when I'm excited by the changes in my life, it still takes time to process the emotions that come with them. I wasn't unhappy, just in new territory again. Should I rush back to Medford to be reunited with my Honda? Or should I continue on with the plans George and I made? After shelling out $390 for the rental car, my analytical side recoiled at the thought of all that additional expense. I had a vision of spending the fall on the East Coast when the trees changed color, then the winter in Key West and the spring back in Palm Springs, but that was too ambitious a plan without a car.

I studied my atlas all afternoon calculating distances to all the places of interest along the way, using various routes back to Medford. I decided that I'd return to Oregon for early fall and then start south to Palm Springs just before winter. I could decide where to go after that once I got settled in the desert. The hardest part of living this lifestyle is deciding exactly where and when I want to travel. Once I've decided on a plan, I settle down and get right into the work of getting there. This time, I wanted to try something different. I would take only two-lane roads back to Medford. I was tired of worrying about what I could and couldn't handle. From now on, I would just do what needed to be done without trying to anticipate the outcome. If a road was on the map, I would assume I could drive it. Maybe I was being unrealistic, and probably that bravado would be tempered by reality over time, but I was having a symbolic breakthrough. I made a conscious decision to worry less and do more.

The next day, I packed a light lunch for a day hike starting just off of Going-to-the-Sun Road at the highest point in Glacier National Park. I wore an old ski jacket, jeans, and a long-sleeved T-shirt. It was already August, and I couldn't imagine being cold at high noon at any elevation. The drive up the road by car was disappointing. After Banff and Jasper, this was pretty, but unimpressive. Was I jaded already? The trailhead was right across from the Visitor's Center, and although the temperature was a lot cooler than I expected, the snow on the trail was packed solid and looked welcoming. Wearing canvas tennis shoes, I set out into the snow. The trail was slippery and briskly cold in the shade. I fell several times climbing the ice-covered rocks, and soon my sweat was adding to the moisture from my falls in the snow. The elevation made every step up the trail, which was now becoming steeper and more slippery, a lung-bursting exertion. It felt wonderful. It was as though I was purging my body of all the mental toxins that were poisoning me. What did I do to make George change toward me? Why did Linda have such an instant dislike for me? Eventually, the climb made rehashing everything impossible. Breathing and moving were the only two messages being transmitted through my synapses, and I felt more energized and focused than I'd felt for weeks.

An hour later, I sat in the sun and ate my lunch. The snow covered mountains that surrounded me, and the reduced oxygen at this elevation, combined with cool breeze, and gave me a euphoric buzz. If my feet hadn't been so wet, I might have continued, but it was time to turn back and get some dry clothes and shoes. When I got back to the car, I stripped off my wet clothes and changed into my sweats, which I had almost forgotten were packed in the trunk for just this kind of emergency. At times like this I had to appreciate some of the good things I'd learned from Don. He was a safety nut. If I went on a two-hour hike, he made me pack enough water for three days, a change of clothes, sweaters, a jacket, dry socks, food, flares, a compass, and rope. My compromise to his excess was to keep all sorts of safety gear in the trunk but only carry water and food and a couple of layers of clothes in my backpack. Today, the change of clothes in the trunk was a wonderful reward after a difficult hike. I took off my shoes and rubbed my cold, wet feet. I liked the sensation of exhausted discomfort. It reassured me that my senses were working and that I was still very much alive.

I spent the rest of the week working out, doing laundry, catching up on e-mail, and cleaning house. There was nothing exciting, just normal day-to-day existence at home with the Rocky Mountains in my backyard. With all the housekeeping done, it was time to hit the road, and Highway 2 beckoned as the perfect two-lane road to cross Montana and Idaho to Oregon. I made a few phone calls to trucker friends to make sure I wasn't going to end up on some bumpy, ill-maintained highway, and got a "thumbs up" from everyone. And it was great advice. Highway 2 goes from twenty-five mph to seventy-five mph as it crests and falls through every small town along the way. There was no shortage of roadside parking and out-of-the-way diners. I didn't let my Sweetwater experience make me cynical and found that it was the exception rather than the rule. The only traffic outside of the towns was trucks, and they were as eager to stay out of my way as I was to let them pass. But my newly repaired cracked windshield attested to the fact that we were all going way too fast. As the trucks whizzed by from the opposite direction doing at least seventy and me in my eighteen-ton Beaver coach doing more than eighty, it felt like I would be shaken right out of my lane when we passed. It only took a few days to get to Coeur d'Alene, but it was my first experience with sleeping in deserted fields, stopping at the side of the road for lunch and dinner, and having no schedule, timetable, or ETA. I never felt frightened, although I did sleep with mace on the nightstand next to the bed, just in case.

Coeur d'Alene was another first. I was treated cruelly by fellow RVers. I was happy to register for a week to catch my breath, have a few good workouts, and decide what my stops would be in Oregon, just a short trip away. Unhappily, the weather was heat stroke hot, but there were two or three hours a day when the sun hit my awning and made a cool, shaded retreat. I was watching the Republican Presidential Convention on television to see who would be Bush II's running mate. While I lounged in the shade, my next-door neighbor came over and struck up a conversation. "So, what do you think of Cheney as VP?"

"I'm a Democrat, so you're asking the wrong person!" I answered jovially, with no rancor, even though I was very opposed to Bush's choice of a running mate.

Actually, I was also very opposed to Bush, but I didn't feel it would be appropriate to say what I really thought. My neighbor didn't smile back. Rather, I could feel him recoil as his body language changed dramatically. He crossed his arms across his chest, straightened up, and took a more aggressive stance. I felt his hostility even though his words still didn't reflect it.

"Are you traveling alone?" he asked.

I quickly quipped, "Yes, I'm on my way to Key West by way of Oregon and California." I laughed at my own witty description and found my new companion was not amused.

"Isn't that where all those 'alternative lifestyle' people go?"

I wasn't sure what he meant, but I was sure I didn't like it. "I guess I'm one of those 'alternative lifestyle' people myself, so it shouldn't be a problem."

I resented this man's attitude, and I couldn't excuse his bad manners just because we were standing in some of the most conservative real estate in the country. I still don't know if he was referring to the large libertarian population, the large gay community, or the huge number of unemployed free spirits, but he was so pompous I couldn't keep my mouth shut. I would come to regret offending him.

A few days later, I was outside in the sizzling sun checking the tire pressure and making sure the various fluid levels were okay when I discovered that my tires needed air. This was cause for celebration, because I had gone to a great deal of expense and trouble to have a fifty-foot hose made to comfortably reach from my coach's built in air compressor to all of my tires. I had even had extenders installed on my inside rear tires so that I could easily check and adjust the air pressure. I got out my handy dandy hose, connected one end to the coach valve, and began to fill the tires. It made lots of noise, but every time I rechecked the pressure, there was less and less air instead of more and more. It was really hot, and enough salty perspiration was rolling down my face into my mouth to remind me to add a little salt to my dinner. As I moved from tire to tire, the result was the same. Each tire got flatter and flatter until it was visibly noticeable. My next door neighbor just sat and watched. Finally, after all six tires on the rig were visibly flatter than they were when I started, he strolled over with no urgency whatsoever and pointed out, "You know you've got to have the engine running for the air compressor to work."

That made sense. I had to have the engine running to fill the airbags, so I politely thanked him and ran inside, put on the engine, and started the whole process again. After trying to inflate each of the tires again, the result was similar, only worse now because the tires were getting dangerously low. Again, my neighbor strolled over, if possible, even slower than the last time. "You might want to put it on fast idle. You know you're just putting the air from the tires into the airbags instead of putting the air from the airbags into the tires." By now, I was really hot. The temperature was about ninety degrees, but after all the physical exertion in the direct sun, my body temperature was probably closer to 110 degrees. I stopped, went inside, and drank some water. I didn't want to ask him how to put on the fast idle. I didn't know there was such a thing and now it stood between me and inflating six flat tires. Once my body temperature came down and I replenished some much-needed fluids to my dehydrated body, I felt better. I went outside, walked up to my neighbor, and just asked, point blank, "How do I put on the fast idle?"

Now was his chance to do with me as he wished. I know in his heart he wasn't evil, but he was standing with a bunch of other men, and I know he was enjoying toying with me. He was the mighty lion, and I was his weak, little, struggling prey. One of the men he was talking to jumped up and started spilling his guts. *Oh thank God*, I thought. *Chivalry is not dead in Coeur d'Alene, Idaho.*

"Use cruise control. Let the coach idle at about 2000 rpm's and you might be able to get some air into the tires instead of into the airbags."

"Wow, I had no idea. Never in a million years would I have thought of that on my own. Hey, thanks."

"Don't get too excited yet. I don't think even that will work. You've got a big heavy rig here, and I don't think your compressor is powerful enough to push air into the tires no matter what you do."

Well that sure took the air out of me. I couldn't think of anything to say for a couple of minutes. My mind was racing. I'd had the hose built specifically for this purpose at the RV dealer who sold me the rig. Why didn't they mention that it wouldn't work? Why hadn't my neighbor mentioned that it wouldn't work before all my tires were flat? What kind of mean-spirited people were they, just because I'm a Democrat? I thanked the man for his input, turned off the engine, and went to the office to get a phone book.

I was going to need a Les Schwab Tire Center, and I prayed that one would be located nearby. As has been proven over and over on this journey, my angels were hard at work, and there was a tire center located just a mile up the road. The question was, could my coach safely travel a mile on such under-inflated tires? I called them up and asked if they made house calls. I was being totally facetious—always the comedian—but the guy on the other end of the phone told me that the truck wouldn't be available until late the next day. I had hoped to leave the next morning. So I gave him the long and short of my story and after a few pointed questions, such as, "How much air pressure do you have?" and "How far away are you?" he suggested that I drive very slowly while assuring me that there shouldn't be a problem. Bless their hearts at Les Schwab. They are really wonderful to RVers. There was no charge and no questions, but the technician who filled my tires did have a puzzled look on his face when he saw how low all six tires were. I was too hot and worn out to offer much of an explanation, so I simply said, "It's been sitting around for a while."

Chapter 21
Reunited with My Car without a Direction

THE DRIVE BACK to Medford was easy and relaxed. I felt in control of the coach, thankful to be on my own, and anticipated getting my car back with excitement. It was clear to me that no matter how much of a hassle towing a car could be, there was no other way to travel. Arriving back at the Holiday RV Park felt like a reunion of sorts. The owners of the park were excited to see me and wanted to hear all about my travels, and when I rejoined the local gym, some of my workout friends remembered me and wanted to hear all of my stories. Of course, it all sounded more glamorous in the retelling.

Each week became more and more comfortable, and the idea of starting a trip to Key West became further and further from my conscious thoughts. It wasn't until another RVer started asking me what my plans were that my mouth seemed to work independently of my brain. "So where ya' headin'?" he asked innocently enough.

"Key West," I answered as though I'd given it a great deal of thought and had already planned my route.

"That's a long way to go all on your own, ain't it?"

And I thought, *Them there are fighting words.* My answer became my next quest. "Not so long. I love Key West. It's one of my favorite places. I can't wait to get back."

And thus, my decision was made. Motivation: ego, the story of my life. I'm always ready to show any stranger just what tough stuff I'm made of whether it's something I want to do or not. But Key West is one of my favorite places, and the prospect of returning for the winter was exciting, so I began to think seriously about what would be required to get there.

I spent a couple of weeks planning the route, checking out the appropriate

RV parks along the way and realized that I'd need to secure a place in Key West now, even though I wasn't planning on arriving for four months. Don and I had stayed at a wonderfully luxurious place with a private wharf, a tiki hut, and double-wide sites that were beautifully landscaped and situated right on the waterfront. I was afraid to find out what the monthly fee would be, as I'd be arriving at the height of the season, but I knew it would blow me away and I didn't care. One voice in my head kept telling me how ridiculous it was to stay at the best place in the entire state of Florida, maybe the entire country, and the other voice was quick to remind me that this might be my only chance to do this. I went with the indulgent voice and booked a site on the water at the beautiful Blue Water Key Resort for a mere twenty-five hundred dollars a month with an intended stay of three months. I decided that this was my reward for getting there, and for following the call of the road. I suppose for some it would be reward enough to eat a big piece of chocolate cake.

Once the deposit for the site was mailed in, I took a few days to let my decision sink in, and then I flew into a frenzy of preparation. The coach was still crammed with stuff from the Oxnard house. The last remnants of things I'd held dear from my past were shoved into every drawer, cupboard, or basement bay. It was time to simplify. I asked myself if I was ever really contemplating going back to my life as a CPA. Did I really think I would ever again sit in a room, hour after hour, day after day, organizing other people's lives? The answer was a resounding no, although the economy would eventually prove me wrong. There was no way to know at that time that the entire country would have a meltdown in just a few short years.

I finally gave away the last of my business clothes, all of the "fat" clothes, and all of my winter clothes. I made a strong conscious decision to never do winter again. And if I did, then I'd just have to buy new clothes. I did retain one coat, one set of long johns, and four sweaters. Next, I needed to confront my horrible rat pack tendencies and consider all the canned goods I would never eat and the three sets of dishes I would never use. By the time I was done, I had made a huge dent in opening up some storage space. Lastly, I had to let go of most of the books I'd already finished reading to make room for new ones. In the old days, I had a library filled not only with current books but also with books I had lugged around with me from as far back as high school. Maybe this was the hardest part of RV life for me—not having room for a library. I was much loved by the local thrift shop that became the recipient of most of my overflow. And in truth, I was relieved to unshackle myself, yet again, from all this accumulation of stuff that had no real benefit to me. I didn't often read books twice, as there were so many more that I wanted to read for the first time. The only thing I couldn't part with was my music.

Greg had taken me shopping and picked out almost every classical CD I had. Nothing else really mattered to me.

I arrived in Medford in early August, and by late September, I was ready to return to Palm Springs. The trip from Medford to Palm Springs was now a familiar drill. I needed to make one stop before proceeding to Cathedral City in the Palm Springs area where a friend had subleased their space to me at a reduced rate. My favorite repair facility had opened a shop in Camarillo, California, right on Highway 101 on the way to the desert. Butch and Sundance were old road warriors now. They kept a running conversation going as we traveled down the road. They would swat at the passing eighteen wheelers through the safety of the windshield, and they were clearly proud of their prowess in keeping us all free from danger.

When we arrived at the repair facility, the service manager and I did the initial walk through. I systematically plowed through my four-page list of repairs until one item, which I'd hoped would be covered under my extended warranty, was debatable, and the manager wanted to see the fine print of my warranty contract. "No problem," I told him. "I know exactly where the paperwork is."

I ran enthusiastically out the door to search through my files in a storage compartment located in an outside storage bay. In my excitement, I left the coach door open. I'd never left the door open before. I guard the door like Momma Bear standing between her cubs and a curious tourist with a roast beef sandwich. But this time, I left the door wide open. My heart dropped through my stomach and landed somewhere north of my shaking knees when I turned around, paperwork in hand, and saw the door just flapping in the breeze. As I climbed back inside, I began to frantically quiz the service manager. "Did you see the cats? Did they get out? There should be two cats in here!"

The poor guy looked horrified. He had been going over the list of repairs and was totally preoccupied with planning my work. After a brief search, I realized they were really gone. "Don't worry, I'll get help and we'll find them." He got on his walkie-talkie and said, "I've got an emergency here. Two cats got out of the Beaver Patriot coach at the entrance of the service department. Anyone who's free, get out here and help us search."

And come they did. We had seven people including myself combing every inch of a huge sales lot with at least two hundred new and used motor homes parked row after row. I couldn't help but think that this was hopeless. The cats had never been outside without a harness. Butch is the adventurous one, and there's no limit to how far he might venture. Sundance was cowardly, and I was even more concerned with how deeply he would bury himself behind or under something to avoid detection by strangers. Even worse, they didn't have on collars and name tags. I had just ordered new ones to reflect my new cell phone number and hadn't received them in the mail yet. In spite of all the help, we were unable to find the cats.

It was getting dark, but I needed to do something, anything. I couldn't just sit and wait. I decided to get my flashlight and walk the entire lot one more time. I walked slowly, examining underneath each coach with my light. About halfway through the lot, I saw a cat. No, I saw two cats. It was Butch and Sundance. Oh my goodness! My relief was overshadowed only by my fear of startling them and having them race off again. How was I going to coax them out? That was a laugh! As soon as they heard my voice and saw my outstretched arms, they made a mad dash up my body and threw their paws around my neck. These weren't small cats. They each weighed in at over fifteen pounds, and holding on to two excited, clawed, fur balls for the walk back to our coach was tricky. I did notice that they were under a Safari model motor coach because I'd traded one in the previous year, and I was familiar with the body style, but I didn't give it much thought. I just wanted to get them home.

The next day while my coach was being repaired, I took a stroll to check out all of the coaches for sale. It's fun to get ideas for decorating and upgrades, and even dream about purchasing a newer model. I came up to the motor home where I'd found Butch and Sundance and stopped dead in my tracks. In the daylight I could see the model and the color. I knew this coach. This was my coach. I'd traded it in less than a year ago in Cobourg, Oregon, over a thousand miles away when I purchased my Patriot. I ran around to the rear to be sure it was really the same one and there it was. The custom mural on the back verified that this was it. Butch and Sundance had found our previous motor home in the midst of close to two hundred vehicles and then waited patiently for me to come home and let them in.

What amazing instincts these creatures have. I suspect Butch found the motor home and Sundance had the good sense to stick like lint on a black suit to his brother. When the repairs were over and we pulled back onto the road for Palm Springs, I looked over at my darling companions. They had already started their usual chatty dialogue as they checked out the horizon for something interesting to scare away.

Once I settled in at a nice Palm Springs RV park, I was ready to enjoy this late autumn visit with my friends. David and Tom, both artists and a very sweet couple, were frequently available for afternoon drives to out-of-the-way hiking areas. We also began taking a nude drawing class. We'd sit for a three-hour session and draw the same model over and over. After about ten minutes, the model changed position, and everyone flipped to a new page until he or she changed position again. It was so much fun, and I even began to show improvement.

It was a season of laughter and the camaraderie of old, familiar friends. As usual, I fell into the routine of knowing how each day would unfold, and I was grateful beyond measure for the consistency. My reservation in Key West was for February 15, and I planned on leaving Palm Springs January 2, thus allowing myself six weeks to meander through the South and the Gulf and see everything of interest in between. We decided that the New Year's Eve party should be a party to end all parties, and it evolved into a progressive dinner event. We'd have a different course at each house, and one designated driver would let us all have a wild night without any danger.

David volunteered to be the driver. The first stop on the dinner route was my place, and I had been assigned wine and cheese. Diane and I had purchased about five pounds of cheese and four bottles of wine, just to get things started. Everyone was supposed to come by at 6:00, and we went out to the picnic table and started nibbling on cheese and crackers and sipping wine, assuming the guys would be along any minute. At 8:00, they came driving up to find us immersed in drunken conversation with about two pounds of cheese and at least one whole box of crackers gone. It didn't take long for everyone to catch up with us, and from somewhere, a very high-quality joint appeared, and the munchies soon followed.

We moved our entourage from my place to Mario's. Mario is a hairdresser who worked in San Francisco for a couple of weeks and then came to the desert for a couple of weeks. With his wonderful Hispanic flare, his home was redecorated frequently, and each version was better than the last. He chose a variety of ethnic delicacies to dazzle our taste buds, and it was spectacular. We ate everything in sight, and when we started groaning about how full we were, another joint appeared, and all complaints stopped immediately. We moved on to Dan's place and were greeted by cakes, candies, custards, fruit tarts, and whipped cream for everything. By now we were all deeply in munchies mode, and we were all good to go for this new round of delicacies. By the time we finished grazing through the sweets, it was nearly midnight. We sat there drunk, stoned, and middle aged, surrounded by a room full of people who truly cared about each other. It was a great moment.

David was sitting next to me, and I was leaning affectionately against his shoulder. I was feeling safe and protected, and the thought of leaving for Key West in the morning was foremost, if not slightly fuzzy, on my mind. I mumbled to David, half under my breath, "I'm scared to death. There are a lot of miles between here and Key West."

David turned to look at me, and I felt how much he truly cared for me. "You don't have to go," he reminded me.

"I know."

"You could stay in Palm Springs," he added.

"I know," I almost whispered.

"Why are you going so far?" He really didn't get it.

"I don't really know. But something is pulling me to do it. Once I get on the road, I know I'll get into it and it will be wonderful. It's just that first step. It's got me scared to death."

David shook his head like a confused parent trying hard to understand what prompts their child to do the strange things they frequently do. He reached over, squeezed my hand, and said, "You'll do fine."

I think we all decided simultaneously that this would be the last New Year's Eve celebration of this magnitude. We were much too old to do this to ourselves. Our bodies just didn't snap back like they used to. At midnight, we turned on the television, waited with Dick Clark for the ball to fall, and as one, feebly blew our horns and shook our noisemakers, and passed out. I vaguely remember David driving me home, and when I woke up in the morning, I was covered in bruises from getting in and out of the van. We never did celebrate New Year's Eve that way again. But the feeling of family, and the security of knowing that no matter what, there are people in the world who care where I am and what I'm doing is something I celebrate every day of my life. This is what carries me and protects me no matter where I go or what I do.

Chapter 22
Key West or Bust

IN THE MORNING I woke up slightly hung over, but absolutely eager to be on my way. I had chosen the easiest route, I-10 all the way east, and planned to take side trips as my courage and progress allowed. Since the weather in Palm Springs was mild and sunny, I didn't give much thought to storms or extraordinary conditions. My blissful ignorance about potential weather disasters was a gift since there were so many other things to consider. It was more productive to worry about the things that were in my control than it was to worry about the things that weren't. It wasn't until I hit New Mexico that the weather took a turn for the worse. Dark clouds began accumulating overhead, and the temperature began to fall. It was obvious that snow was not out of the question. Now there were plenty of things I was willing to try, but driving in a snowstorm was not one of them. I pulled into an RV park that was rated as barely okay, but I didn't have too many choices. All of the parks in the vicinity were right off the highway, and they were all just parking lots with hookups.

When I checked in, I was comforted by the friendly ambience and cheerfulness of the office and the proprietor. I had arrived just in time to sign up for dinner, which was a private affair for the guests who chose to eat at the park. Since there were no restaurants for miles and unhooking the tow car in the upcoming storm was unappealing, I paid my six bucks and signed on. Dinner would be in two hours, which gave me time to get settled in my space, take a shower, change clothes, and join my fellow wanderers.

At the appointed hour, I approached the dining room feeling shy and keenly aware that everyone's eyes noticed that I was sitting down to eat by myself. I chose a table with an older couple of my parents' generation. They seemed less isolated, and even a little welcoming, and there was an empty chair. "Do you mind if I join you?" I spoke in an uncharacteristically shy voice.

"Oh no, of course not!" came a jovial response with a heavy German accent. "We have plenty of room for such a charming young woman."

The accent caught me a little off guard, although I was accustomed to endless German tourists at the various RV parks. They generally were very young, usually in their twenties. I had never met anyone from Germany who was my parents' age and quite possibly survivors of the war. I was very careful to avoid the subject, as I really didn't want to know what they had been doing during WWII, and my biggest fear was that they'd tell me.

Once the food was served, the wife began telling me her story. She had grown up in Germany during the Hitler regime, and she described how difficult life was for her and her family. I bit my tongue so hard, I was almost gagging, but when she started talking about what a good job Hitler did, except for "that Jewish thing," I almost bit my tongue right out of my mouth.

"Excuse me, but what do you mean, 'that Jewish thing'? That was the main focus of the Third Reich. Don't you consider that to be rather significant?"

"That's only one small part of what Hitler stood for. He made the economy work. He put us back to work. He put food on our tables. Yes, what he did to the Jews was not a good thing, but he was going to save Germany."

"Not a good thing? It was more than 'not a good thing.' It was a heinous thing. It was an evil thing. You make it sound like he levied an unfair tax or something."

My blood pressure was climbing, and no confrontation was worth having a coronary, especially because of some pathetic Nazi sympathizer.

"I'm sure you'll understand if I don't stay for dessert." I stood up and left the eating area and stomped back to my motor coach. I don't know why the opinion of one ignorant woman hurt me so much, but I cried for all the people who died because people like her thought it was "not a good thing." I rummaged through my jewelry case until I found my Star of David I'd bought at least twenty years ago on a visit to Israel. I put it on and have not taken it off since. The storm came, and rather than snow, we were given a thorough drenching with an electrical light show with angry thunder, which closely matched my own state of mind. And then it was over. I pulled out in the morning still a little shaken, feeling unwelcome, and questioning what I would find in the South. My next major destination was New Orleans, and I arrived in plenty of time to find my RV park in daylight. When I visited New Orleans two years earlier with Don, we stayed at a park that was way outside of town, and this time I chose a park that was closer. When I arrived, I realized that I couldn't make the turn into the driveway. It was situated right next to a small, crowded gas station, and the park entrance was partially blocked. If I tried to turn left into the park and avoid the illegally parked car, I would block oncoming traffic and quite possibly have to get out and disconnect the car while blocking the highway. Having been there and done that, I decided I would just continue on and hopefully pass another RV park.

No park materialized, and when a sign leading me back to the freeway appeared in front of me, I had to make a decision as to whether I wanted to drive around New Orleans blindly looking for a place to land or if I'd be better off getting back on the freeway, stopping at a rest stop, and calling ahead for a new place and be sure I had specific directions. I opted for the latter. Before I knew it, I was in Mississippi when a rest area finally presented itself. I got out my trusty *Trailer Life Directory* and found an RV park that had space for me.

I was way ahead of schedule, having skipped New Orleans, but I was looking forward to getting to the powdered sugar beaches at Panama City on the gulf coast of Florida. Dan had spent a lot of time there as a kid, and he described it in such a way that it sounded like someplace to stop and enjoy for a week or two. I was ready for a rest, as I'd been driving three to four hundred miles a day, and I'd just about had all the driving I could take for a while.

Nothing eventful happened during that two weeks in Panama City Beach, and I had earned it. I was still so intense when I drove and terrified whenever I had to get fuel or turn off the beaten path that much of the pleasure of this life still eluded me. I amused myself by surfing a couple of the singles sites on the Web every chance I had, and I was now corresponding with several single men that I was planning to meet as I got closer to Key West. I don't know why I persisted in dating men from the Internet, since I had met my last husband and Don that way and they both had ended badly. But ever the optimist, I persisted in this non-rewarding behavior. I had corresponded with what seemed to be a nice Jewish doctor. He was in Hollywood, Florida, and this would be my last stop before I headed south to Key West. If we hit it off, he lived close enough to visit me, and miracle of miracles, he had a motor home and he was retired. This was the closest to a potential partner in crime that I'd found, and I was looking forward to meeting him. We'd talked several times on the phone, and he sounded sweet, kind, and thoughtful.

The trip across Florida by way of Alligator Alley had lots of places to stop, and nearly every place had wild birds or alligators or something worth seeing. I was finally beginning to enjoy myself. I stopped at a state park with a sign posted as I pulled in, "Beware of the alligators." I didn't really think about it but knew if I was confronted with one it would definitely be given the right of way. I went about my business of hooking up and as the door slammed behind me, it apparently didn't click shut. When I came back from my hookups, the door was wide open and Butch was gone. Now this wasn't like getting loose in a residential RV park. This was a park filled with protected alligators. Even worse, next door there was a huge dog, and he would certainly make it difficult for Butch to come back, especially if he started barking.

While I sat on my step trying to decide what I should do next, I saw Butch run out from under the coach. He'd been sitting behind the front tires. He stopped momentarily to sniff some errant blades of grass in the otherwise sandy park, and I had to act in a moment or all would be lost. I dove at his tail, which was the closest appendage within reach, and slid into it as though it were home base and I was scoring the winning run. Just as I grabbed his tail, the dog began to bark and the cat began to run. I was on my stomach, face in the sand, my hand firmly on his tail, and held tight. Eventually, I was able to pull him in as though I were reeling in a fish, and once I could get a grip on his body it was all over. I don't know if there were any alligators nearby. It was enough that there could have been. I'm not sure which of us was more shocked. I'd never in all his life pulled him with all my might by his tail. Maybe he felt my angst or maybe I just scared him to death, but regardless, escape was no longer an issue between us.

My next stop was Hollywood, Florida, and I'd be staying at another state park very close to where my new doctor friend lived. When I arrived, it was filled with weekend campers, and there weren't any other huge coaches there. The spaces were small and cramped, and I'd gotten the picture that most state parks are not geared to accommodate my size coach. But I made do and settled in, and when it was time for him to come meet me, I was as nervous as a schoolgirl.

On the road, I had the opportunity to date—I mean dating like you're supposed to do in high school. I'd taken advantage of the opportunity to explore different personalities and types of men and in an adult way realize that just because a man loves me, desires me, or wants to be with me doesn't mean that it's the best decision for me. All of the dates had been respectful. I learned what I probably should have learned thirty years ago, so meeting the doctor was really just another date. He turned out to be a very nice man, just too hyper and unable to sit still for five minutes. He drank heavily and smoked marijuana endlessly. I'm not a prude, and I don't really have an argument with social drinking or even social marijuana use, but to date someone who is self-medicated from the time they get up until the time they go to bed is just not interesting. I think it might have been more about his inability to adjust to being retired than that he really had a substance abuse problem. He had been a successful, busy doctor for years, and now he didn't know what to do with himself. Oh well, he sure did look good on paper.

A sign warning to beware of alligators where
Butch decided to explore on his own

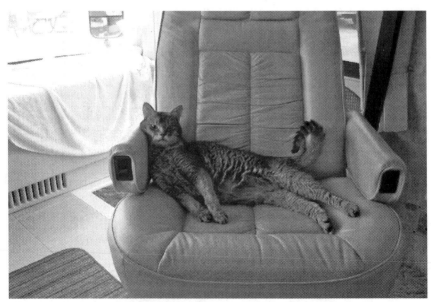

Butch relaxing in his easy chair, May 2006

Chapter 23
A Letter from the Morgue

ONCE I ARRIVED safely in Key West and settled in my amazing site, I did all of the things that I was accustomed to doing regardless of where I was. I found a gym with yoga classes. I figured out which were the best music bars on Duval Street to hang out and sip iced tea while listening to the various bands. I even made a few local friends. I was looking forward to three months of exquisite paradise.

Within a month or so, while I was going through my mail, I noticed a letter from the Wayne County Morgue. I ripped it open quickly and found that my sister had died. A neighbor had identified her and was able to locate my most recent address from Gail's phone book. The letter went on to explain that Gail was being held at the morgue waiting for instructions from her next of kin as to how to dispose of the body. By the date on the letter, I calculated that she had been in the morgue for over six weeks. I couldn't get to a phone fast enough. I called the morgue and identified myself and explained that I would get there as fast as I could get a flight. They did what they could to calm me down and assure me that now that they knew I was coming, there was no hurry. *No hurry?* I thought. *My sister has been on a morgue slab for six weeks, and there's no hurry? I don't think so.* I hung up the phone and called my cousin Jack, who lives in a nearby upscale suburb of Detroit. He's an attorney, and he'd know what to do.

"Jackie, it's your cousin Patty."

"Patty, it's been way too long. How are you?"

"Jackie, Gail's dead! I just got a letter forwarded to me that she's in the Wayne County morgue. I don't know where to start. I called the morgue and told them I was on my way, but they want the name of a mortuary where they can send the body for preparation for the funeral. I have no idea what to do."

"Patty, it's okay. We'll use the mortuary I used for my mom, and we'll bury her at the same cemetery my mom is at. I'll have a rabbi from my temple perform the service. I can get everything started, so that by the time you get here, we'll be nearly ready. Patty, I'm family. We'll take care of this. Call me as soon as you have a flight, and I'll be at the airport to pick you up."

I breathed a sigh of relief. I had so little family that the gentle reminder that as small as it was, it was still family and still there to help, gave me comfort. I went to each of my nearby neighbors, knocking on their motor coach doors, until I found someone at home. The first two coaches I approached were both occupied by very elderly people. I just apologized for the interruption and continued on to the next door. Eventually, I found someone who was actually enthusiastic about taking care of the cats. I ran back home, packed, called the airline for a ticket, called the airport shuttle service, and it seemed that within an hour of getting the letter, I was on my way to the Miami Airport. Once we took off, I took a deep breath and tried to relax. I let my mind wander over my relationship with my sister. What a roller coaster ride that was.

While I was living in Europe, I was out of the loop when it came to all of the family drama surrounding Gail and her illness. I left my mom to do whatever she needed to do, but I really didn't want anything to do with it. Once Gail started living on her own, my mom moved to Hawaii and then San Diego, probably with as much desire to escape as I had. Left to her own resources, Gail was able to buy a HUD house for twelve thousand dollars in the most distressed area of the inner city in Detroit. When I was married to Jørn, we had visited her. That's when I saw how she lived. I remember that we arrived at her house, and I was surprised at how small it was. When she opened the door, the sight was too much for me to take in all at once. The house was filled with huge bags of cat litter. They were everywhere. Every inch of floor had bags stacked as high as possible. Apparently, she had somehow found a bargain and had a ton of litter delivered to her door. The house was filled with the odor of cat urine, testifying to the presence of too many cats in too small of a space. It was enough to make my eyes tear. Jørn was amazing. He spoke kindly to Gail and conducted himself as though this was the most normal home he'd ever visited.

In addition to the cat litter, my sister had her four-room house filled to the brim with junk and trash. I'd heard of pack rats before. I was even guilty to some much lesser degree myself, but I'd never seen anyone at this advanced stage before. I forced myself to sit down and carry on a conversation. In spite of the fact that we hadn't seen each other for years, we had spoken on the phone every week since I'd returned to the states with Jørn. She was my sister, and I loved her. The environment she was living in appeared to be a fire hazard and a health hazard. I focused on her face rather than look around at the contents of the house. But that was heartbreaking, too. She was emaciated at around eighty pounds and was dressed in old, ripped clothes. She spent most of the visit telling me that her neighbors wanted her dead, and that they all hated her because she was a Jew.

Her speech was affected and slurred, primarily due to the shock treatments she had received while incarcerated in the mental hospital for her various attempts at suicide. Her brain, in a word, was fried. She wasn't taking any medication, and that was apparent from her disjointed story lines. She spoke of one friend across the street who visited her regularly, and I said a silent prayer of thanks that someone was kind enough to reach out to her. She spoke in the vernacular of black slang, reflecting her social world, and after about an hour of conversation, I felt that if I didn't leave, I would faint from the smell of urine and spoiled garbage.

She was a paranoid schizophrenic, and most of her story of danger and intrigue was only in her head, but as I sat on the plane, I knew that she hadn't been completely paranoid. A few years earlier, she had been raped in her home, and she had called and asked me to install bars on her doors and windows. The house next door was a drug house, and one of the men high on something had broken in and raped her. Her solution was to ignore my offer to move her someplace safer, but instead she bought a dog. Of course, I had someone install the bars. They charged twice the normal rate because the neighborhood was so dangerous that they feared for their lives as they drove there to do the installation. I was happy to pay whatever they asked.

Many years later after my father died, while I was married to my third husband, I again tried to get her to move to anyplace she chose outside of the inner city. I only asked that we find homes for all but two of her cats so that we would have a chance to find a landlord that would accept her. I knew there was no chance if she insisted on taking all eight cats. My husband offered to go to Detroit to get her, find an appropriate house to rent that was in a safer place, and to help her get moved and settled, and that's when all hell broke loose.

He had mentioned to her in a phone conversation that he had lived in the Synanon community many years ago. Gail decided that he had brainwashed me with drugs and that he was coming to get her and kill her. She extrapolated that he had murdered his sister and now he was going to murder her. She wrote me a long letter forgiving me for my part in the planning of her murder, but nonetheless, she was having nothing to do with us moving her to a new location. She confided to me that she knew I was the devil, and at least once a week she began leaving amazingly complicated messages on my office answering machine accusing me of the most heinous things. At first my secretary dutifully wrote down every word Gail said, such as, "Tell Patty I know she's the devil and that I'll never let her get away with killing me," until experience taught her to pull out only the important part of the call, and I'd get a note that simply said, "Gail called, and she wants a refrigerator." or "Gail called and asked for food." I would send whatever she asked for, but I couldn't call her back. It was just too painful. And now, I wished I had found a way to convince her I wasn't the devil. At that time and place in my life, I just didn't know how.

Once I arrived in Detroit, my cousin picked me up at the airport. I stayed with him and his wife while we handled the planning of the funeral. Over the years, Gail considered herself an Orthodox Jew. She didn't go to synagogue, and she didn't keep kosher. I don't know by what criteria she placed herself in that category, but when I planned her funeral, I kept that in mind. The traditional Jew is buried in a plain pine casket. When I looked at the caskets with the silk and the fine expensive wood, I consulted with Jackie and he encouraged me to do what I thought was right. I chose the plain pine box. The Mortuary consultant was appalled, and you could see the judgment on his face. I ignored him and honored my sister. Then he offered an additional option for an extra five thousand. He explained that we could have a cement wall built in the gravesite to protect it from water damage. That one really threw me for a loop. She's dead. Her body is supposed to decompose; dust to dust, right? When I told the man under no circumstance was I going to build a cement protective barrier, he stopped trying to sell me extras and we concluded our business.

The funeral was attended by Jackie and his wife, and a couple of second cousins and one other first cousin. Also, the neighbor that had befriended my sister was there, and a wonderful female Rabbi did the service. After the funeral, D, my sister's neighbor, called me over and asked if she could speak frankly with me. She was distressed and nervous, and I couldn't imagine what she could possibly have to say that would be so difficult. "I was the one who discovered your sister's body. When I found her, she was on her hands and knees with her behind up in the air and her clothes pulled down to her knees and it looked like she had been raped. They said she died of a heart attack. I say she died of a heart attack while she was being raped."

When I got back to Key West, I called the coroner's office every day, and every day I got the run around. Finally, weeks later, I spoke to an actual person. I insisted that they send me a copy of the autopsy. They refused but said that she died of a heart attack, and that's all they could say. I asked if they had done any tests to see if there were any evidence of sexual activity, and they said there was no reason to. And so, I had to let it all go. There was nothing to do. She was dead. No one would ever be punished. And whenever I think life is too much of a challenge, I think of Gail, and I wonder how I would have handled living a life filled with all of the real and imagined demons she had to confront every day of her existence. I doubt if I could have done better. It was never easy being Gail's sister. But in hindsight, I realize it was a lot more difficult being Gail.

Chapter 24

The Family Plot and the Evil of Greed

THE BI-MONTHLY MAIL was always filled with a few surprises. I would get delinquent bills that had slipped through the cracks, invitations to events that had taken place a week or two before I received the invitation, or news of business transactions that needed immediate action but were already out of date. As I opened my mail, my eyes were immediately drawn to the letter from an attorney. After the letter from the morgue, I knew any official notice was a potential bomb. It had been addressed to the beach house I sold just before I hit the road. It had been forwarded twice to various RV parks, and finally it was sent to my mail forwarding service. I opened it warily, wondering if I was being sued for one thing or another. But it was worse.

The letter said that my small lot in Polson, Montana, was being sold for three years' back taxes of a whopping $180. This was the lot that my father had purchased with his fellow school bus drivers in 1954 for $500. After my father died, I tried to get the attorney who was handling his estate to transfer the title from my father to the estate. Unfortunately, the attorney in Nevada handling everything was either having a nervous breakdown or he was a criminal. Either way, he was unavailable 100 percent of the time. In fact, his staff treated my phone calls as an interruption to their day, and no one ever returned my calls.

I called the Polson, Montana, property tax people, and it was amazing. A person spoke to me immediately, understood the problem, presented a solution to me, and handled the transaction over the phone. The attorney who was handling my father's estate had neglected to pay the property taxes for a few years. I explained to her that the only way I learned of the delinquent taxes was because I got a letter from an attorney stating that he was buying the property for the amount of the back taxes. If that letter hadn't been forwarded to me, I would never have known there was an issue. I wonder how many properties were lost in just this way. The attorney who was going to buy it was a predator. I was beginning to think he was working in cahoots with the estate attorney who wouldn't take my calls. First he lets the land go into default, and then his cohort buys it up for a few pennies on the dollar.

She suggested that she immediately change the address on the account to my current address and that I pay the delinquent taxes by credit card right then while she had me on the phone and the default sale would immediately terminate. She handled everything. Although the sale was stopped, she explained that I would need to hire a Polson attorney to get the property transferred since the estate attorney was incompetent. I explained that I lived in a motor home, and it would not be difficult for me to drive over there and handle the whole process in person, especially since I was only six hundred miles away. And now that the department of revenue knew that the property was being transferred, they would keep an eye on it and make sure there wouldn't be any transfers until I had a chance to deal with the issue.

When I arrived in Polson, I found that solving the problem wasn't going to be as simple as I'd hoped. I met with an attorney who explained that they had to go to court and make the request formally for the current attorney to transfer the land. If he failed to respond, then they could appeal to the court to let my new attorney handle it, or something to that effect. It was going to cost a minimum of nine hundred dollars, and possibly more. But then that would be that. Although I wasn't sure why I even wanted the property, in my heart I knew that it was all I'd ever really have from my father. I admit to some sentimentality.

Before I decided if I wanted to spend nine hundred dollars to save a five hundred dollar piece of land, I went to one of the real estate offices in town to see what the market value actually was. The agent and I took a drive and found my parcel was part of a wild wetland. All of the adjacent lots belonging to the other bus drivers and their families were under water. My lot and the lot next to me were the only dry ones. I had no idea what the lot was worth, but even more than that, I had to ask myself what I'd ever use it for. Eventually, I would have to sell it to someone. I knew I wouldn't live here because the winters are brutal and I wouldn't visit because I had absolutely no friends or relatives in the area. And then, when I asked the agent how much it was worth, he said it would probably appraise out at ten grand. He asked me why I didn't just donate it to the local Indian tribe. I'd get a tax deduction, and they'd be able to get it connected to the other lots as protected wetlands. It would be a "win-win" situation.

Except, he let it slip that he was very involved with the tribe, and I got the impression that snagging a donation of this particular land would somehow be a good thing for the tribe. I decided if it was good for the Indians, it was good for me. I would hold the land and hire the attorney to get it in my name before I left Montana.

The attorney explained each step and how long it would take. He suggested I go on my way and take care of signatures by mail or, in most cases, by fax. And it all went according to plan. After twenty years as a CPA, you would think it wouldn't be a surprise to me to find a professional who is able to do a professional job, but I was just as surprised as I was relieved. Within a few months, all the paperwork was handled, the court date had come, and everything was completed. I now own a small lot in downtown Polson, Montana. It was anticlimactic when all was said and done, but I felt that the forces for good had prevailed. Ironically, a couple of years later, a shopping center began planning a project that would border on my property and property values would soar. Even with the depressed economy and the decline in property values in 2008, the last appraisal was for over fifty thousand dollars. So for once, it could be said that good triumphed over evil.

Chapter 25
The Story of B

THE DEFINITION OF insanity is doing the same thing over and over and expecting a different outcome. But Internet dating is like a drug; there's always the possibility of finding an instant connection. To be able to shop for a relationship in the same way that you would shop for a television was tantalizing. You choose who you want from a menu of traits and then look at pictures for the proper visual, and then voila! It was perfection. It was happily ever after.

After all this time on the road, I'd finally begun to define myself as single and capable. I didn't go whining for help every time something broke. I sat down and tried to fix it by myself, and if everything else failed, I hired someone, but not before I'd given it everything I've got. I had traded in the 1995 Safari Continental thirty-seven foot motor coach for a 1998 forty-foot Beaver Patriot. The Patriot was a beautiful specimen. The previous owner had put in every extra available. I had a dishwasher, clothes washer and dryer, two satellite televisions hooked up to "in motion" satellite, and plush padded wall coverings. Even though the cats did do their damage now and then, for the most part, I took exceptional care and repaired everything the moment I had an opportunity either to figure it out or hire someone. It seemed that most of my travel revolved around repairs, and I was beginning to tire of the continuous stints in the repair bays of RV facilities around the country. I was hungry for the emotional and physical intimacy that comes from connecting with another good soul.

Since I currently had limited Internet access and using snail mail seemed more convenient, I changed tack and ran a singles ad in the *Trailer Life Magazine* and received hundreds of letters in reply. Each reply was amazing.

I received letters from almost every state and several from prison. Each story was more touching than the last. Widowers who poured their hearts out to me in loneliness and sorrow begged for an opportunity to meet me and travel with me in my motor home. Even then I knew I wasn't looking for someone to join me in my motor home, but more precisely, I wanted someone to travel in their motor home and caravan with me in my motor home. They were tall and short; they were thin and thick; they were foreign and domestic; they were smart and dumb; they were every religion and every culture. But there was no chemistry with anyone. They were either too old or too young, and some were just too scary. And then I came to B's letter. He had attached a picture of a sculpted young man on a sailboat and a head shot that was ruggedly handsome. His letter said:

> Dear Pat,
>
> I was intrigued by your ad in the *Trailer Life Magazine* personals. I was so impressed with your lifestyle. You must be a very strong, independent woman, and I find that very attractive. I realize that you want to meet someone with a motor home, but I have a feeling that we will hit it off and make whatever compromises we need to so that we can get to know each other. Please call, write, or e-mail and I will respond immediately! Until then,
>
> B

My first thought was, *How full of himself is he?* That then ran full speed into, *What kind of compromises does he think I'll make? Maybe he's just looking to move in with me. Maybe he wants someone to move in with him.* Eventually, I stopped speculating and wrote all of my questions to him. Let him tell me what he's looking for. He's the one who's asking me to be interested in him. Let him tell me why.

> Dear B,
>
> Thanks for your e-mail address. I just bought a new contraption that AOL has just come out with. It's able to send and receive e-mail wirelessly, and it's small enough to hold in my hand. It doesn't receive attachments, but the text will all come through, and it's instant, just like regular e-mail. Your letter intrigued me. But I am left with more questions than answers. Since I don't plan on stopping traveling, and you don't plan on getting a motor home, what kind of friendship/ relationship do you envision having with me? As it turns out, I will

be in Morro Bay for the winter. I'm taking some classes at the Jewish temple in San Luis Obispo, so we will have some time to get to know each other if we decide there's some reason to do that. I'll be arriving in a couple of weeks. Let's start out with a cup of coffee and go from there.

Pat

And so when I arrived in Morro Bay, he was already there waiting for me. Boy, what a challenge that was. As I pulled into the RV park with my forty-foot coach with the appendage of my 1998 Honda following obediently behind, my adrenalin was pumping, and my entire being was on full alert. I had to perform my duties in order to get settled into a space. Finally the levelers were down, the slides were opened up, and the engine was shut down. I looked over at B, who had jumped inside the coach as soon as I arrived and observed the entire procedure. I broke the ice by saying, "That's one tough way to meet someone. I can't imagine what you must be thinking right now. I'm really quite a girlie girl, but not when I'm operating this rig. It's not that easy to navigate, and I have to have my focus 100 percent on what I'm doing."

B's face lit up when he smiled. His face went from ruggedly handsome to just plain handsome. "Pat, I'm in awe. Are you joking? I didn't find it unattractive at all, if that's what you're worried about. You're amazing. You handle this thing like a pro. I've never seen anything like it. I'm ready to marry you on the spot!"

We both laughed as we drove off in his car for a local restaurant and that cup of coffee. We talked for hours, and by the time he took me home, we felt like old friends. B respectfully dropped me off and asked if I'd be around the next evening. When I told him I was busy, we spent some time negotiating a next meeting in a friendly, easygoing way. This was going to be a good winter.

B and I had a five-year relationship that was always easy going and fun. When I was in town, we always spent as much time as we could together, and when I left, there were no accusations or guilt trips. To the best of my knowledge, B was a solitary man living out in the backwoods in the outskirts of Morro Bay, California, and surfing every free minute he could find. I enjoyed my time with him and I enjoyed my time away. For all those years, I never gave much thought as to how he amused himself while I was gone. We were in constant touch by e-mail, and as lovers often do, we shared intimate thoughts and sometimes rather sexual musings. One winter, B wrote that he was finally ready to join me on the road. We would maintain our separate RVs and sometimes travel together and sometimes go our separate way. The arrangement suited both of us, and I was very excited about this turn of events. It was so unexpected, as he had always been very clear that he loved his solitary life and had no intention of changing. I was always very clear that I loved my life on the road, and I, too, had no intention of changing. For five years, this seemed to suit us both.

As the time drew closer for him to join me in Lake Tahoe, our e-mails became more and more sexual as we anticipated getting together after an absence of several months. The morning of his departure he wrote:

> Hey there sexy, I'm just going to ride a few waves this morning before I leave for Tahoe. I can't wait to see you. This has been a long time coming, and I finally know what I want, and it's you.
>
> See you very soon,
>
> Love,
>
> B

The time came for his expected arrival, and I didn't hear from him. This was not like B. After all the time that we'd spent together, we were both very reliable in our comings and goings. When we had plans to see each other, we were excited and happy, and we both showed up on time with big smiles of anticipation. This was very weird. Several days went by when finally I got an e-mail from B's e-mail address. It was a response to my previous, very explicit description of all the things I was going to do to him once he arrived:

> Pat,
>
> You don't know me, but I'm B's girlfriend. We've been together for the last six years. I live in Santa Barbara, and he comes to stay with me nearly every weekend. B died several days ago while he was surfing. He had a heart attack. By the time the medics came, he was gone. When I went into his computer, I found all of your correspondence with B. I never knew anything about you, and his last e-mail to you nearly broke my heart. He never gave me any indication or warning. I felt I should tell you that he's gone. I really have nothing else to say to you.

I sat and looked at the computer screen for a long time before it dawned on me that the intimate e-mails B and I had been exchanging in anticipation of his arrival were there for all to see. I wanted to respond to her, but I certainly didn't want to continue the current e-mail thread. I started a new message and responded:

I am so sorry, both for your loss, and for mine, but even more for your discovery of my relationship with B in such an awful way. B spoke of you often, although he told me you were his ex-girlfriend. I would like to at least visit his grave and say good-bye. Could you tell me where he will be buried? I won't come to the funeral, as I don't think my presence would be good for either one of us.

Pat

She answered back immediately:

Pat,

B's ashes were buried at sea in accordance with his wishes. The memorial was on the beach and written up in the local newspaper. I'm still in shock about everything.

And so it ended. No chance to say good-bye. No opportunity to publicly mourn. Nothing remained but the sounds of the lake, the birds, and the cool breeze. Life always seemed to be filled with so much disappointment. I looked upward and shook my head. I didn't cry. It wasn't until years later that I actually allowed myself to grieve for B. It took some time to forgive him, and then it took some time to stop wondering how I could have been so stupid. And it took some time to just let it all go.

Skipping rope outside my coach at the Morro Dunes RV Park in Morro Bay

Before my first surfing lesson at Huntington Beach, California

Chapter 26
Intimacy

I SAT LOOKING at myself in the mirror. *It's not so bad,* I thought. *I'm still okay, especially if the lighting's good.* Thinking of my childhood, playing for hours, making faces in the mirror, I relived the fascination of examining every crease, line, and pore in my face. It distracted me from what was really bothering me. I was painfully, frustratingly, and unrelentingly horny. I hadn't been with anyone since B died. I was afraid to start anything new. I carried a lot of sexual baggage of shame and guilt from old parental reproaches and learned at an early age that sex was bad and that meant I was very bad because I enjoyed it so much.

The television flashed an advertisement for an "intimate relationship" Web site, and I tore myself away from my self-examination to think about the premise. Could I do it, I mused? Could I go online and say this is what I want, and this is how I want it? The thought cracked me up, and I amused myself with answering my e-mail and put my mind on wisecracking with my friends. Before I logged off, I thought, could it hurt to just take a look at the site? Hell, I'll just browse some of the profiles but not respond to anyone. Of course, the web master was smart enough to require anyone browsing the site to have a profile of their own on file.

"Shit," I muttered, but before long, I was totally immersed in creating my own sexual profile. This is amazing. What are my sexual preferences? Do I like leather ... domination ... threesomes ... phone sex ... computer sex? Ex-husband number three would have loved this site. I involuntarily exhaled as I noticed I had been holding my breath for what felt like ten minutes. I felt excitement start to pulse through me, and if I was frustrated before, I was now in a state of agony. Once I finished my profile and posted a few pictures, the messages started filling my in-box. Guys of all ages, all sizes, all interests, and all sexual preferences were vying for an opportunity to do whatever I wanted.

"Hi beautiful," one wrote.

"Hello," I responded.

"Would you be interested in a threesome?" he asked.

"No thank you. I'm looking for a partner. I just want one person, but thank you for contacting me," I replied politely.

"Okay, if you change your mind, be sure to let me know."

I glanced at the indicator showing that there were forty-seven messages waiting. *Good Lord, this is crazy*, I thought, but nonetheless I continued reading them one by one and politely rejecting each one for one reason or another and was even more surprised at how politely they accepted it. Occasionally I "spoke" through text messages with a few men who sounded interesting, but it always turned out that they were in Nova Scotia or London or some other faraway place. Eventually, I was exhausted and signed off completely frustrated but puzzled and curious. The next night I signed on again, and with a bit more experience, I was able to handle over fifty messages when I was contacted by a man who sounded very interesting. After some introductory bantering he wrote:

"I like your profile."

"Hang on, let me check yours."

I expertly flipped over to his profile and caught my breath. He was darling. He was handsome, clean cut, young, in great shape, and really sexy. And he was local. *Okay*, I thought. *Am I playing for pretend or am I in this for real?* I came back to respond to his message and decided to just go for it. I wrote:

"You're really sexy."

"So are you, beautiful," he responded immediately, and continued. "I like that you're just looking for friendly sex with no strings attached. Do you have a really strong sex drive?"

"Extremely strong," I answered simply.

"Do you have multiple orgasms?"

"I do with the right man. Yes, I think so. I have had, maybe not recently."

Well, that was a bit more direct than I was expecting, but the truth was, I wasn't sure. I'd had lovers both inept and magnificent, and B and I had had five years to work things out, but now I wasn't sure I was still orgasmic at all.

"I promise I'm the right man for the job. Can I have your phone number? I'd like to call you."

"That's fast. I've only been online twice for an hour or so. I didn't expect things to move this quickly."

"May I have your phone number?"

After giving him my phone number and getting offline, the phone rang almost immediately. I answered, "Hello." When I heard his young, masculine voice, I felt myself relax at least a little bit.

"Hi Pat, I'm very impressed with your courage to just tell it like it is. Your profile is perfect. I'm looking for someone who wants to play with no romantic nonsense. I like older women. They know what they want, and they aren't all hung up and repressed. I promise I'll satisfy you like you've never been satisfied before. Let me come over and meet you."

I just stared into the phone, half-expecting a hand to reach through the receiver and grab me. I couldn't think of anything to say. He broke the silence. "Hello, are you there?"

"Yes, I'm just a little nervous. Would it be too trite to say I've never done this before, and that I'm actually a little scared? I've done online dating before, but this is not in any way similar. And the men are always twenty years older than their picture, and about fifty pounds heavier. And more to the point, there are no expectations of having sex. Are you sure you look like your picture, because if you really do, you're adorable. But if you don't, well, I'll be pissed."

He laughed audibly. "Honey, I promise you won't be disappointed. Just give me a chance. I need a woman who has a strong sex drive, and you're beautiful. I'll have you screaming with pleasure."

I took a deep breath and said, "Okay."

I gave him directions to my place, wondering if this was my last irresponsible act on earth. What in the world was I expecting? I didn't have long to wait. He was at the door in a matter of minutes, or so it seemed.

In reality it was a couple of hours, but I was paralyzed and hadn't moved a muscle since I hung up the phone. As I walked to the door, my gait was more in keeping with someone going to the gallows. I opened the door to a man in his forties with a boyish face that was made even more youthful by his shy, embarrassed grin. All of the sexual frustration I'd been harnessing for the last six months came gushing to the surface, tempered only by the fear of what I was going to do. As I opened the door for him, I saw that he was visibly relieved to see me too. We made small talk, and I offered him a glass of wine as I poured one for myself, more to kill some time and quiet the voice of reason that was shouting in my head.

It was obvious he'd done this before. He didn't make any move toward me. He leaned back on the sofa and talked about his work, the weather, my home, my animals, and anything that didn't relate to sex. He made me laugh, and I observed myself examining his face and body and was starting to feel drawn to this man. He was sweet, restrained, and surprisingly respectful. I was completely thrown off guard by his sincerity. No line, no story, just a nice guy who wanted to have very wild and uninhibited sex.

As I laughed at his jokes, I found myself touching his shoulder or making a gesture that ended with my hand on his arm. He responded ever so slightly and leaned a bit closer when he spoke. But he did not make a move. I realized that he was leaving it up to me. He was going to be very sure this was consensual, and I was touched by his approach. If anything was going to happen, it was going to have to be my doing. I slowly leaned forward and touched his lips with mine. I was on fire and so scared I could hardly breath. We sat and kissed slow, sensual, teasing kisses until we needed to either stop or go get on with it.

"Do you want to go into the other room?" I asked.

"Absolutely," he quickly responded.

We walked into the bedroom, and he helped me take off my clothes and then took off his. There I was, naked with a stranger. The blood was pounding in my head, but as he touched me, the blood began pounding in a more sexual place, and I lost all sense of time and space as he expertly brought me to orgasm after orgasm. He used his tongue and his fingers, and he responded to my body's every movement. He read my mind. He read my body. And finally, when I was sure I would never have another orgasm, he entered me and it started all over again.

We got up after a short nap, and I asked if he was hungry. I made dinner, and we talked intimately and easily. After dinner and after the dishes were put away, he asked me if I'd like to play some more. I could hardly believe that my body was capable of any more, but when he took my hand and led me back into the bedroom, I astounded even myself as I felt my body become excited again. There was a more relaxed atmosphere this time. I knew that I could expect to be fully satisfied, and I didn't feel the need to rush anything. But my body had a different agenda. I was immediately in spasms of delight and insatiably screaming for more. *Geez,* I thought, *I'm taking him prisoner. This is too good to believe. He's got to finish and then murder me. And right now, for more of this, I can live with that potential outcome.* I never said my priorities were mature. By the time we finished, we both fell into a dead sleep and hardly stirred until morning. I woke to feel him fully aroused against my back, and when he was sure I was ready, he entered me again. What a way to start the day.

I hadn't expected him to spend the night or for that matter to have more than one go round at sex when he could easily have slipped out the door to never be seen again. Instead, he was gracious when I told him I had a 7:00 a.m. yoga class. He asked for directions to the nearest Starbucks, handed me his business card, and said, "I definitely want to see you again. This isn't just a one-night stand. I'll call you and e-mail you. We'll get together again soon." We kissed good-bye, and he gave me that grin of his and thanked me for a wonderful time. It's obvious that I'm attracted to a man's smile. But it's not just that. There's a certain intimacy that a man can communicate with the way he smiles. It's that grin that says, "I see inside your soul." It's a grin that says, "I see you and like what I see."

I closed the door and looked at his card. Yes, he had a name and a phone number and a job. And he'd disclosed it all to me. *What's the catch?* I wondered. I put the card away and ran to my yoga class. I hadn't felt this relaxed in ages. If I never saw him again, well, I'd had the night of a lifetime. And if I did see him again … I would just be grateful. Two days went by, and I was just starting to wonder if it had all just been a quickie, well not so quick, but a one-night stand. And then I heard my computer chime, "You've got mail." I glanced over at the computer and saw an e-mail from lover boy.

You are one hot woman. I'm looking forward to getting together again. I'll be out of town for a few days, but I'll phone you when I get back. Stay hot for me!

I heaved an audible sigh of relief. I half expected to never hear from him again, in spite of the fact that we made beautiful music together, to put it mildly. But one never knew. The Internet is filled with people who say one thing, do another, and don't mean either. I noticed that my whole demeanor was different now. I felt sexier, worked out harder, ate better, and slept less. I knew somewhere down the line this would end and I would feel a sense of loss. But for now, I decided to live in the present and not make it any more or less than it was. What a joyous adventure. There's a lot to be said for two consenting adults.

The relationship lasted for quite a while. We were both honest and open, and when he eventually met someone his age that he wanted to have a relationship with, he told me. We had a fond farewell, and I will never forget him. Many years later, I got an unexpected e-mail from him, asking if I was still interested in getting together with him. It didn't work out, but it still brought back vivid memories and a big smile.

Chapter 27
Debbie, Death, Obligation, and Courage

I HAD BEEN corresponding with Greg's surviving sister, Debbie, while I was on the road, and she had been diagnosed with a rare kidney disease coupled with colon cancer, which morphed quickly into impending death. Coupled with a variety of bad habits, her life was precarious to say the least. When I arrived back to the Newport Dunes in 2006, I was there to prepare for my upcoming December bat mitzvah. Although a bat mitzvah in Jewish tradition is usually celebrated by thirteen-year-old boys, the modern movements of the sixties had brought girls into the ritual. Since I had turned thirteen before this practice was universally embraced by the more liberal streams of Judaism, I decided that this undertaking would be an amazing intellectual and spiritual challenge to achieve as an adult. I was studying primarily on my own, with the occasional help from a tutor and the cantor.

Since I knew how sick Debbie was, I wanted to spend time with her, especially since her entire family lived in Utah and I had an ongoing close relationship with her dad and stepmom. Our history went all the way back to 1980 when I first met Greg and Dan. The day I arrived in Newport Beach, I got word that she was hospitalized. We hadn't had the opportunity to even go to lunch before I was thrown head first into making a decision as to what and how much my involvement would be. I chose to be her advocate. I felt Greg's invisible arms around me and his quiet expectations that I would do whatever needed to be done.

I went to the hospital and continued to go every day for the entire summer. Because of her illness, we spent most of the time in the hospital with her throwing up, or in surgery, or hallucinating or any other number of extreme and heartbreaking events. At first the doctors would always ask who

I was, and Debbie and I would respond that I was her sister, but after weeks and weeks of my being there, they eventually stopped worrying about who I was and accepted that I was family. By the time she was released, it was clear that she was going home to die. In keeping with her desire to die at home, I was happy to continue helping. This was fine, except I was unable to take on the role of nurse, and Debbie needed assistance all day and all night. Her insurance covered visiting nurses, but she was far beyond the need for an occasional visit. She threw up constantly, she had uncontrollable diarrhea, and she was unable to satisfactorily clean herself. I trembled as I called her Dad in Utah and begged him to either come himself or send one of the brothers, but there was absolutely no way Debbie could care for herself.

In response to this turn of events, one of her brothers came, and we did what we could to make her comfortable. Several of her girlfriends brought food and visited regularly, and it was a testament to human nature to see how many of her friends pulled together to be sure food was available as we continued our vigil. An ex-boyfriend of hers showed great loyalty by spending many nights with her and helping as much as he could when he wasn't at work. Eventually, we were called upon to change her diaper, clean her vomit, and watch her die. When things had reached the lowest ebb, and her dad and stepmom had arrived to help with the last days of trying to ease Debbie's discomfort, my life was complicated one morning when my beloved Butch was unable to stand up. He was over eighteen years old, and age had taken its toll.

I woke and was getting ready in a rush. We expected Debbie to die at any moment, and there was Butch looking up at me, unable to move. He was dying, too. I had to choose. Go to Debbie or stay with Butch. I picked up my precious boy, and we took the drive to the vet where I had to have him put down. No time to think. No time to grieve. I just had to decide, and he could not be left alone to die while I was out taking care of Debbie, and I couldn't stay and hold him and comfort him while he died a natural death. I don't think there was ever a more difficult decision. I wanted to just bury my face in his fur and find that old comfort I always felt at his body's perfume. Instead I held him as they put him to sleep. I said good-bye, kissed him, cried, and then drove to Debbie's to watch her die that very evening.

Shortly after her death, I had my bat mitzvah. Experiencing such extremes in so short a time etched both experiences deep in my memory. As is the case with all bat mitzvahs, I was required to lead the service, chant from the Torah, chant the Haftorah, and give a speech explaining how the portion I had chanted applied to my life. I remember how ironically appropriate my Torah portion was. In short, Jacob had travelled to Heron where he was visited by angels. Jacob tells God that if he will care for him, feed him, protect him, take care of his needs, and bring him home safe, then he will believe and accept him as his God. I had been traveling for ten years, and I was tired. I had been kept safe through all of my hare-brained adventures, and each time I thought things couldn't possibly take a turn for the worse, they usually did, but not before I had a good portion of fun and maybe even learned a lesson or two. I was home at least in the sense that I had found a connection to my Jewish roots. I had discovered a spiritual connection, if not to the conventional image of God on a throne ruling our every move with a shake of his fist, but at least a newfound sense of my own divinity and my own power to shape the world for good by simply choosing to be a good person.

Dan and Debbie before Debbie's illness

Chapter 28

Free at Last, Free at Last, Oh
Dear Lord, I'm Free at Last

AND THEN THERE was M. My relationship with him wasn't really a failure. It never really happened. The entire relationship took place in my head, which in fairness wasn't always all that bad. I met him on a singles Web site called Plenty of Fish. He was Jewish, handsome, educated, single, and lived eight miles from my San Juan Capistrano home. Now, this added up to a big fat ten. I had sold my motor home and gone back to work as a CPA part time due to the horrific economy. My life savings had dwindled to an amount that was more than most people would ever have, but not enough to live the rest of my life without working. I was now very involved in the Jewish community, making new friends, volunteering, and living an average, stable, run-of-the-mill life.

I bought my house when I had become engaged to a man who ultimately chose drinking over me. But for three years we had a lot of fun. I was sad when it ended but not devastated. I had loved him but not desperately or deeply. His drinking was always an issue and always something that held me back from giving 100 percent of my heart to him. But it was a comfortable match, and he was easygoing. He accepted my friends, and as long as I didn't give him too much grief about his drinking, he would go along with just about anything. I'd never been in an intimate relationship with an alcoholic before. I didn't quite understand that when they say they will stop drinking, they aren't lying. They just don't have the ability to actually do it. I believed him, time and time again, until I just couldn't stand the sight or smell of him.

After I asked him to leave, I felt relief. I was living in a wonderful community at the top of a hill with a beautiful view and the sweetest neighbors and friends anyone could hope to find. I landed in a good place. I even found work locally at a CPA firm where I was free to come and go as I pleased. I worked two or three days a week and made just enough money to support my frugal lifestyle. I had developed a simple, non-materialistic way of being in the world, and it seemed to suit me. The only thing missing from my life was a long-term companion. I felt I had finally reached a time in my life that I was ready to make that kind of commitment. Once again, I found myself on the Internet. There really is no other way to meet singles. After all these years, the dating sites have become a mainstream way to socialize.

M was my first connection after my broken engagement. I had planned on waiting six months to date, but after five, I felt I was ready. We had an immediate connection when I met him for coffee. He was open, funny, understanding, compassionate, tender, present, and very eager to be intimate. He put me at ease. He had me at hello. He was so easy to talk to. We had so much in common. He had been on a bus with rock bands doing the sound for years. I had been in the motor home for twelve years. We were the same age. We both loved animals. We both didn't have children. He was educated and successful, and he was so cool to be with. We came back to my house, and he proceeded to spend several hours satisfying me. I did nothing but lean back and accept pleasure. And he was a potential boyfriend, not just a playmate. I had been celibate for five months, and I had been reluctant to start a relationship until I had completely healed. And after five months of occasional drunken phone calls from my ex, the sensation of loss quickly healed, and I was relieved that I was no longer locked into an existence of spending the rest of my life watching him vegetate on the couch.

When M and I were finished, he said he had to run home to take care of some things, but he'd be back for dinner. After a couple of hours, I got concerned. I got a weird e-mail from him with some work notes. It was cryptic and didn't really make any sense to me, but after several hours and several unanswered e-mails, phone calls, etc., I gave up and realized he wasn't coming back. The next day I tried finding him, mainly because I wasn't sure if he was dead or if this was some kind of sick joke. I "googled" him and left messages at all of the phone numbers listed online. I got his father at the address he claimed was his home. It was my first inkling that this had been a one-night stand and I'd been had.

It was the first lie. He didn't live where he said he did on his profile. I couldn't believe that we could have spent an afternoon with such joy and passion and fun and then have him disappear. I was crushed, angry, hurt, and humiliated. I had been open and honest and as transparent as a piece of glass. He was a lie. He was a secret. And I would have done almost anything to see him again. He had caught my imagination. And imagination is something of which I have a huge supply. I was depressed and disappointed for a few weeks, and finally when I had just gotten him out of my mind, I got a text message: "Are you horny yet?"

I was incredulous that he would contact me again and pretend that nothing had happened. I answered, "How could you do that? It's been weeks since I've heard from you. You left and said you'd be right back and then you disappeared for weeks. How could you?" I couldn't help ask the same question over and over again.

He texted back, "You called my dad, and you went nuts. I sent you an e-mail so you would see that I was working and you'd know I was busy."

His behavior over time actually got worse, if that's possible to imagine. I resolved that I'd never see him again. I responded to his insensitivity by blocking his e-mail and sending him hate-filled messages. And every time he came back, I saw him. I was caught up in believing that nothing could be that good and not be real. I was convinced that eventually he would understand that we were perfect together. It never changed. He'd come over and be about as charming as a man could be. We'd have the most incredible sex you could imagine, we'd talk, we'd hold each other, and invariably he'd make some mention of arranging to get together in the very near future, and then I wouldn't hear from him for weeks.

I had varying degrees of anger, hurt, humiliation, despair, and indifference, and filled my time with occasional dating, seeing friends, and work. And always there would be the unexpected text message. It was always crude and always sexual. "Do you want to get hot?" I'd be at work, minding my own business and then, always after an extended absence, there would be a message from M. In the initial months, I was always either in a state of ecstasy or rage. He would tell me, "We'll evolve," and "My work is secret." Unfortunately, nothing evolved. And I think it's the first time I really understood my ex's addiction to alcohol. It doesn't matter that you want to quit. It doesn't matter that you know it's the best thing to do. When the glass of wine is sitting in front of you, nothing can keep you from taking that first sip. And then finally M confessed. He sent me a long e-mail explaining his behavior

Patty,

When we met, I had been in a seven-year, on again/off again relationship with someone from _____. It was, at that time, off again. Without getting into a long-winded story about that relationship, its biggest problem was lack of passion (more like a sister than a lover). I tried to never see you both. I am monogamous by nature, and like you, I don't cheat. It seemed like every time you and I would get together, she would find a way to get back into my life and I could not see both of you. Then she would make it clear to me that it was over and I would see you. Then she'd reappear, begging to try again, so I would avoid you. Obviously, I was a coward and not honest to either of you, although I never saw you both in the same time frame. Additionally, your expectations would run ahead of our relationship. In my attempt to not hurt you by having you fall for me and then me having to say that I was going back to my old girlfriend, I would avoid you. Now, however, she is complete history. It is a long story that I would share, but I don't type very well, and it is a burden to relay things in this media. I will gladly discuss them, however, verbally. So, I have no satisfactory excuse for my behavior, only an explanation, but not an excuse. There is no promise of where our (yours and mine) relationship could go, but I believe it would nourish itself. Want to try, fine. Want to play until we find new mates, fine. Want to be nonsexual friends, fine, but I'm not certain that we could pull that off. Want me to really get lost, just say so, I will respect your wishes. No argument here, just this. You might actually like me. However, in the meantime, we live nearby. We love sex with one another. We love to talk, make out, etc. So, until you see that I am not the asshole that I have you believing that I am, we could be friends who have fun and whatever. It's your call. I am off until Saturday if you are so inclined.

M

M,

I'll be brief. I finally get it. No more fantasy, just the truth. You are a coward. You caused me depths of pain that you will never understand. You lacked the courage to be straight with me. Everything that's ever passed between us has been delusion on my part. Okay. I'm no longer delusional. Every word we've shared, every touch, was tainted with cowardice and lies. I'm choosing to never see or hear from you again. Go back to the other woman. I deserve so much better than you. This has nothing to do with sex, other men, or anything like that. You lack character. And I only just this minute came to realize that's what it is. I'm actually 100 percent over you. And unlike you, I won't stand you up. I won't lead you on. I won't deceive you. I just don't want you anymore. Good-bye. I don't need to block your e-mail or avoid you. There's no reason. You can write, call, text, or anything else you may want to do. Wow. Free at last. Dear God, I'm free at last. Karma is tough. You made your bed, now you get to lie in it.

Patty

My rabbi said that resentment is like taking poison and then waiting for the other person to die. We can spend our lives resenting every real or imagined wrong, or we can take every experience, and value it for the lessons learned. Good people make bad choices, and bad people sometimes choose to do good deeds. Life is about the journey. Where we land doesn't matter, because it's sure to change. What matters is how we got there. So what now?

I must ask myself some hard questions. Do I want to get married? Answer, no. Do I want to live with someone? Answer, no. So what is this incessant need to be tied at the hip to another person all about? Does it all come back to the never-ending societal dictate that we must all find happiness in the Ward and June Cleaver fantasy? For those people who truly want that, they should be free to pursue that path, but what about those of us who for one reason or another are more fulfilled pursuing a more solitary path? Of course I understand the need for the family unit for raising children, but for a mature woman whose eggs are way past the expiration date, why must I aspire to what I don't really want?

The answer is so simple. I can't believe I've spent my life searching for the Holy Grail of happiness to find it's already mine. I want deep and honest friendships, monogamous and exciting sex, challenging and fulfilling work, intriguing and fun hobbies, and freedom to have as much or as little of each as I choose. And I already have all of those things in my life.

What now? I will make wiser choices and never stop living life as an adventure. At Greg's funeral, a representative of the Mormon church came to the mortuary to speak. Greg had been excommunicated because he was gay, so the service couldn't take place at the church. He noted that Greg brought to mind the famous words, "To thine own self be true." These are powerful words coming from a Mormon clergy in reference to an excommunicated member of his flock, especially since he was excommunicated precisely because he chose his truth above all else.

May those be the words on my tombstone, and may I live a life worthy of them.

My last RV before hanging up my traveling shoes – a
2005 Dutch Star diesel pusher with four slide-outs